Recalling Past Life

About Days Forgotten, Dreams Dreamt, Books Read, and Some Flute Music

by Franz Rothe

1603 Capitol Ave., Suite 310 Cheyenne, Wyoming USA 82001
1-888-980-6523 | admin@urlinkpublishing.com

URLink Print and Media is committed to excellence in the publishing industry.

Published in the United States of America

Library of Congress Control Number: 2023911525
ISBN 978-1-68486-453-9 (Paperback)
ISBN 978-1-68486-456-0 (Hardback)
ISBN 978-1-68486-455-3 (Ebook)

26.06.23

Contents

Preface

This booklet is for entertainment. It dates back to an era almost bygone before the pandemic and flood and fire disasters struck worse than ever. The freedom of writing something as irrelevant and idle as this booklet is now absent. So my exchange of ideas was fading out for the past three years. While I reread the careless, partly lost notes that had been sent to relatives and classmates a long time ago, I noticed the recurring willingness to answer. Retired because of my poor eyesight, my interest in literature had awakened and the exchange seemed worthwhile once more. Thus this little booklet has still been gathered. My heartfelt thanks go to everyone involved, especially Hans-Peter for his constant attention. Charlotte , May 2023.

Keywords: school memories, literary criticism, humor, cat love, philosophy of mathematics, flute music, dream experience, Kafka.

Genre: entertainment literature, flute literature.

About the author:

Franz Rothe graduated from high school in Karlsruhe and studied mathematics, physics and music there. Graduated with a diploma in mathematics from the E T H Zürich, a doctorate in Tübingen. After some changes in life, a professorship at the University of North Carolina at Charlotte, USA. In addition, Rothe and pianist Thomas Turner have developed a repertoire of classical music for flute and piano, and have recorded and released three CDs. This collection also contains several of their own transcriptions. Now Rothe is retired and keeps writing books about mathematics, and too, just for entertainment.

Remark. This English translation has been corrected and slightly extended. The older German version of this audio book, together with some music is available at Amazon and other places either as one long mp3 file, with the cover depicted on page 6, or in three separate parts either as mp3 or wav files.

Tagesreste

Teile I, II und III

Erlebtes, Ertraeumtes, Erlesenes, und Floetenmusik   Franz Rothe

Part I

Short Episodes

I.1 First Ideas, Mostly Cheerful

I.1.1 My Cat

With the computer I copy the synopsis of the book,
which pretends to be so utterly important,
Meanwhile you tip over the glass of water
on the table with your front paw.
I cannot but laugh.
You retreat to the cardboard box in the corner,
turning your back on me.
A black stripe of black fur,
right and left I see, somewhat irregular, dazzling white.

When I look at the black spot on your right hind paw,
    only the right one,
my love is renewed by itself.
You only eat the cheap canned food
    and lick the carpet fibers.
You've been vomiting twice already.
The red spots on my arm,
will you bite again tomorrow morning?

I.1.2 It Should Have Been Simply a Walk

Five minutes by car from my house, near the Hilton Hotel,
a pretty artificial lake has been laid out. The place is popular
for relaxation and is visited by many joggers, pedal boaters,
and walkers. Now some land around the lake has been sold, and
apartment complexes are to be built near the bank. A high wire
mesh fence from the road to the shore incloses the construction
lot. The old buildings inside are demolished. I recently went
back to look if at least a poster with information about the
current developer has been set up. On my way, I remember
that my three house-plants are still in the small shop next door

because of my trip two weeks ago.

I am going to pick up the plants. As I enter the shop, I see a customer receiving her plant and paying 20 euros. I give the waitress my slip. She brings a cardboard box, on the edge of which my three plants are squeezed into plastic sleeves.

"95 euros."

"But it only costs 20 euros per plant."

"But your plants were in public space and have been badly damaged."

While I want to explain that she has damaged the plants, I already rummage in my wallet. There are only 20 euros bills. I want to give her five bills.

"It costs an additional 20 euros exchange fee."

I'm digging again. Suddenly, there are many one euro bills, they are a little smaller, completely worn out, and printed with black ancient ornaments.

She doesn't take them. I search and search. A wind comes up. The whole kiosk drives and I sit in it with no roof above. I put the bills sorted into several piles, somewhat protected from the draft. There is a 150 euro bill and some a little newer black 15 euro bills. I've never seen these bills before. With some counting, I can perhaps get closer to the sum. The kiosk continues to move past some trees. After five minutes, the journey goes backward, hopefully back.

I put a thick pack of one euro bills into a bag. Then the other bills into another bag before all the money is blown away. After paying, I leave the kiosk carrying out the three plants and look for my yellow car. I shall never again enter this kiosk.

I have to turn my car. It only works if I drive down a small path. At its end, there is a place with gravel and sand piles. Now I see a lot of children's cars there. The children happily drive up and down the gravel and sand piles. There is hardly any space to safely turn my car.I get out and pull the car back and forth several times with the tow-rope. Finally, the car is turned, and I could almost leave the gravel site. A four-year-old arrives in his toy car and stands up in front of my right front wheel.

"Could you please move aside?"

"This is our playground." The boy got up and falls over with his toy car, right in front of my wheels. With the help of the tow-rope, I have to pull my car back and forth several times. Fortunately, that works.

Finally, I have arrived at home and still want to wash my feet. With my wet feet, I am standing in front of the sink and looking for a towel. Only in the closet next door there is a dry one. The cat lies picturesquely stretched out on the tiles in front of my feet. I can't move a single step.

I.1.3 The Cat Is Injured

My cat is still doing badly. She is just coming and settles herself on the keyboard, asking me what I'm doing here. She also wants to jump on my lap. I can feel that she has a fever again. I can now see the bad wound on the left hind leg. It still doesn't heal well. Everything happened last Tuesday. May be, she was so badly frightened by the road works that she jumped through a broken glass window into an uninhabited house in the neighborhood. Anyway, it has happened last Tuesday morning. In the evening I saw her again, but I still didn't know about her wound. That gave me a greeting by a bad scratch. For a week now, the animal has only been living in my house. If she were healthy she would have plagued me long ago, and meowed until I open the window, and she was gone again just for one day, sometimes two. When will such a life come back? Now her accident is eight days ago. After I come back from the merchant this morning, she has disappeared, but there was only a small gap open at the top of the kitchen window.

Yes, the cat came back afterward. She hadn't hurt herself again when she was squeezing herself through the narrow window gap. Usually I left a lower window open for her, and only stuffed in a pillow. Then she always came back at different times of the day or night. Finally, a badger or other clever predator noticed the trick, broke in at half past two at night and tore open several coffee bags. Otherwise nothing happened, the badger has simply disappeared.

I.1.4 Plato and Slavery

The professor has been lecturing for half an hour. Now both blackboards are fully covered with his notes. He picks up the eraser and hesitates.

"In ancient Athens, there would have been a slave for wiping the blackboard." It slipped out of him like that.

By the way, do you know that Plato sailed to Sicily three times, with the intention of founding an ideal state there? The third time, he meets the tyrant Dionysus. Some historians speculate he had promised to come back. Now he has just explained his plan to the tyrant.

"So you tell me that in your state, every man and woman does the work for which they are best suited."

"Yes, Mr. Dionysos."

"Let's see." The tyrant approaches Plato and grabs him a bit at the upper arm. "Healthy guy, strong muscles."

He explains: "It is really convenient that my large slave market will open just tomorrow morning. Water carriers are urgently needed for my thriving economy. We will offer you immediately on the right side at the entrance gate. Excellent sales prospects! And before the sun is high up at noon, you no longer need to make push-ups. Then you can do something more useful."

And whether Plato's friends had listened right behind the door and were able to free him on the spot, or whether they only bought Plato free on the slave market the next morning, this is not known. In any case, Plato and his friends managed to sail back to Athens. And only after his attempt to establish an ideal state had failed for a third time, did he found the academy in Athens. It developed to the first university.

"And did he continue to advocate slavery afterwards?" asks a student in the back row.

"So little has been handed down safely from ancients times. But I think, yes." The professor answers and begins to wipe the blackboards.

I.1.5 Become a Plumber!

Once upon a time, there was a professor of mathematics. He was doing quite well, except for a little something that bothered him at home. All the water taps dripped and dripped. He had already wasted many a free hour trying to remedy the defect himself, now he was fed up and called a plumber. The handyman was able to remedy the defect very quickly, to the satisfaction of the professor. At least until the plumber finally scribbled some almost illegible characters and numbers on his notepad, and handed the note over to the professor. He looked at it and was horrified.

"That's a third of my monthly salary."

"Lord, then they come to us and become plumber."
The professor found the proposal worth considering.

"I just have to tell you one more thing. The masters with us do not like educated apprentices, and often do not take them at all. So it's best to say that you only have seven years of elementary school."

With determination, the professor goes to the master. And lo and behold, the trick with the seven years of elementary school works. Now he goes to the plumber apprenticeship three times a week. He can already cut threads and even measured the thickness of a pipe correctly. The journeyman's examination will soon be passed. A new life with more money is waving soon. And that brings advantages.

But after a year there is another obstacle. The guild of North

Carolina artisans has decided: all artisans should be better educated. From now on, all plumbers in the state of North Carolina
need eight years of elementary school. If you don't have that,
you can catch up on the eighth school year in evening courses.
Our professor alias plumber journeyman must now go to school
three times a week in the evening.

The first lesson is on mathematics. The teacher comes in.

"Hello guys. I want to see what you know so far. Tell me,
what is the area of a circle."

Silence. "It is round."

The teacher distorts his face. "But how big is it?"
An awkward silence again. Finally our professor lifts his hand.
He has forgotten, but can derive it. Whether he should come
to the blackboard. Yes, so he goes to the board and starts to
calculate: [1]

> Integral from r to minus r   over the root of r-square
> minus x-square de x
>
> is equal to integral from r to minus r   fraction r-
> square minus x-square over the root of r-square
> minus x-square de x
>
> is equal to and so on...

The professor continues to lecture: "The next step is to separate
the integral into a sum of two integrals, and then one needs an
integration by parts."

The formulas become longer and longer, the teacher becomes
anxious and more anxious. Some of the schoolboys have already
fallen half asleep, others grin with malicious glee. But the professor does his job and at the end of the calculation he gets
"minus pi times r-squared half." $(-\pi r^2/2)$ But that's not what

---

[1]
$$\int_r^{-r} \sqrt{r^2 - x^2}\, dx = \int_r^{-r} \frac{r^2 - x^2}{\sqrt{r^2 - x^2}}\, dx = \ldots$$

one expects. The professor sweats, and even the teacher sweats a little bit. Finally, one agrees that this is only the area above the x-axis, and you have to add the same area below the x-axis. So you get the double, which is "minus pi times r-squared." But that's not as expected, either. The professor sweats even worse, and the teacher almost gives up. Finally, the smallest guy answers from the last row.

"One should swap the boundaries of the integral, and calculate integral from minus r to r."

Bad tongues claim that the professor got a D and the clever brush an A in math. And so the professor is still a plumber today. But the guy, yes, that's a different story.

I.1.6 Knecht Rupprecht is Late on the German Railway

Knecht Rupprecht's account has been cracked. The little lad has just hardly slipped away, there the train was gone. His red coat has remained on the platform. Did anyone find it? Knecht Rupprecht fell asleep on the train and the hat was also stolen from him. He arrived in Sulzburg only in his undershirt, I have heard, gray and dirty.

He rang the bell at Dean R. Sündno 's. The children had just started practicing Schumann's "Knecht Rupprecht" on the piano. Knecht Rupprecht brushed off his gray shirt as best as he could and apologized. (See the picture Hans-Peter has of it, and that this booklet shows to the valued readers, too.) The piano playing reminded him of the slow rumbling of the slow train. Being asked, where he was coming from, they should tell him, but they had to remember for a long while.

"Once too late, and everything for the cat" he said angrily.

"Knecht Rupprecht, you have read too much "the country doctor", Kafka is not the right literature for you. I also hacked your account and have seen it exactly."

Einer geht noch!

The parents stand there silently and look at each other with embarrassment. We couldn't find out what else happened to the Sündno family afterwards. The bug that Knecht Rupprecht left behind had unfortunately been delivered from China and sent the reports to the law firms there.

Footnote. It is a working principle of the authority that error options are not expected at all. This principle is justified by the excellent organization of the whole, and it is necessary if the utmost speed of completion is to be achieved. ☐

But I remember hearing Dean Sündno 's voice:
"Have pity and understanding, and pray for servant Rupprecht!"

Post scriptum. The Kafka quote in the footnote is the first in the collections to find good quotes and best quotes on the Internet.

Every child knows the beginning of the poem:

> From outside I come, from the forest;
> I have to tell you, it is very Christmas!
> Now speak how I find it in here!
> Are you a good child, are you an evil child?
>
> —Theodor Storm

Hanno writes he can't find them, these interesting YouTube videos where Schumann's *Knecht Rupprecht* is really badly mis-played on the piano. They may already have been deleted. However, I only searched a few short addresses. But google something like this:

Knecht Rupprecht by Robert Schumann, from *Album For the Youth, opus 68.* □

I.1.7 Musil's Törleß on the Theater

A theater adaptation of the "Young Törleß " was to be seen on stage in Mainz, with a woman as director and with women in the leading roles. Even the trailer shows the striking style aimed at excess, everything stylized and abstract to the extreme. On the contrary, the mastery of the novel lies in describing the dangerously slow way in which the young pupils ("Zöglinge") are drawn step by step into the whirlwind of masochism and sadism, medieval hypnosis, and more strayings. Smart actors are needed to slowly increase the tension. They act in and as the center, they are the most important part of the performance. Too much artistry, distorting speakers, and more of the like, all that only distracts the audience. I have already observed similar defects when comparing two versions of Dürrenmatt's physicists: broadcast on television in 1964 on the one hand, and with Herbert Fritsch in 2015 on the other hand. In this case, too, one can see how the artistry takes over, thus pushes back, and meddles with the content of the piece. I now understand why Dürrenmatt turned away from the Zurich theater, becoming rather disappointed towards the end of his career. After a long talk, the reasons are becoming apparent during the discussions with Ludwig Arnold.

It takes a lot of skills to show both strands of the Törleß novel: on the one hand, the confusion that mathematics creates in Törleß as soon as you think beyond the small multiplication table,—on the other hand, the extremely strong relationship between Törleß and his mother. This unhealthy bond also favors perversions - sadism, masochism, even including homosexuality. Puberty and growing up are for the youngsters always cause both cognitive and emotional problems. Stressing this double challenge is for me the essence of the novel *"The Confusions of the pupil Törleß "*.

It becomes obvious how dangerous both incomplete knowledge and bragging are, especially during puberty,—how they favor latent mental disorders and cause them to break through. Can you convert "The Young Törleß " into a good play that shows the above processes even more emphatically than Schlöndorff's movie? It would need a master to do this.

Here are a few lines as a first humble beginning of what I intent.

Teacher: Today, I want to explain the imaginary numbers. The idea is very simple. We just pretend there is something like "the root of minus one", and we use this object as a unit of account.

Törleß: Teacher, but there is no root of minus one at all.

Beineberg: It doesn't matter, we just pretend it exists.

Teacher: Beineberg always participates well.

Törleß: Sir, may I write my formula onto the blackboard, it confuses me. Everything is correct, but why is it not working?

Törleß writes on the board: [2]

---

[2]

$$-1 = (\sqrt{-1})^2 = \sqrt{-1} \cdot \sqrt{-1}$$
$$= \sqrt{(-1)(-1)} = \sqrt{1} = 1$$

minus one equals the root of minus one squared is equal to the root of minus one times the root of minus one

second line: is equal to the root of in brackets minus one times minus one is equal to the root of one equals one.

Törleß: In the end we get that minus one equals one. But we know that this is wrong.

Teacher: Later you will understand all of this. Now it's just a matter of believing that it works.

Reiting: Caesar says: the first line is allowed because I saw it, allowed it, and won. The second is forbidden because it brings us to the deepest Germania. It must never be written down again.

Beineberg: No, I have to see what's on the board. How the roots touch, loop around one another, and unite. I have to go right through this struggle. That is my way.

Basini: If someone simply takes a euro away, it won't be right, either.

Next appearance. Already on their way, they talk to each other.

Reiting: I am lacking money and Basini reveals himself.

Törleß: But he's so honest.

Reiting: I really think Basini took a euro out of my drawer. He wants to distract us. Otherwise, he wouldn't have talked about taking away a euro.

Beineberg: The interrogation in the little closet will be our pleasure.

Törleß: What do you find out. You won't be able to calculate and build bridges.

Bozena: Look, how cute boys are coming! But why so excited, did the teacher confuse you once more?

Beineberg: It is not his profession to show how the roots unite.

Bozena: With me, you are at the source. Not only roots unite here.

Basini: My whole family comes from noble roots. When we all gather, we fill a large hall.
Beineberg: I just want you. The unification needs practice and concentration.
Bozena: For the beginning, the boys may get some tea and rum. Well, fresh up!

I.2 Tübingen, an Important Station

I.2.1 Excellent Behavior

From the long years as an assistant at the institute of Professor Karl-Peter Hadeler, also called KPH, I remember only few critical remarks towards to me. Admittedly, more than I want to frankly mention here. He liked to call me "Emperor Franz" and warned me not to exaggerate. A reminder that the scientific career must move forward quickly was often due.

"Everything takes forever with you."
The most violent remarks I remember are:

"I am still your employer" and "You are really a strange person."

By the way, I remember an anecdote that KPH once told at the institute tea. At the train station, he had just helped a young lady and carried her suitcase. Where does she want to go? To a congress for teachers of German and German scholars. German was KPH's favorite subject at school alongside mathematics. For whatever reason, he took his time and stayed at the conference for the coffee break. With his good nursery, he has just joined another participant, introducing himself as Dr. Hadeler, and a conversation started. They are talking about the relationships between Goethe and Riemer and between Goethe and Eckermann. Out of genuine interest, KPH contributes some details. His counterpart is pleased with the stimulating conversation and the two gentlemen have a good time with each other.

Until the conference participant asks what he is currently working on. KPH replies that he is a graduate mathematician and an assistant in Hamburg. The conference participant hints another greeting with his hand and says:

"Dr. Hadeler, I am very pleased to have met you," gets up and leaves.

I.2.2 Remembering Karl-Peter Hadeler

He left us on February third, 2017. Beginning September 1973, Prof. Dr. Karl-Peter Hadeler had been my doctoral supervisor, and two years later for many years my employer at the University of Tübingen. Because of the overwhelming expectations and the strangeness I experienced at the E T H, and the imminent death of my father, I had not been quite happy during the past time. I was new at in Tübingen. Always since the start of my dissertation, Hadeler has been an always reachable contact person for me. For example, Hadeler had translated for me important publications by Kolmogoroff et.al. from Russian and had spoken them on tape. Soon I got to appreciate the hospitality of Helgard Hadeler and her family. Thanks to all their friendliness, I felt much more at home than I had in Zürich during the years before. Hadeler's chair for biomathematics had a circle of long-term and short-term employees. The seminar for biomathematics brought many contacts and constant motivations for my work. Despite this diversity, Hadeler has always encouraged me, as well as the other coworkers, above all to publish independently, starting in small documented steps. Hadeler himself contributed regularly to the work of the assistants.

Over time, it became clear to me that it was the tasks of two professorships that Prof. Hadeler wanted to fulfill and could achieve. In addition to the professorship for mathematics, especially in the Russian school, a second one for mathematical biology, especially in its current developments. Only a first-class man with his exceptional intelligence, perseverance, and human prudence could cope with such enormous demands. It is not the place to pinpoint when I realized the scope of his tasks outlined above - nor how far or not I ultimately have exploited all these options for myself. After 1990 I had to leave Tübingen. It should therefore be left to better experts to appreciate Hadeler's later achievements. It should only be mentioned that in April 2017, Springer's book by K.P. Hadeler on cellular machines will be published posthumously.

I.2.3   Dreaming of Tübingen

What do we not all experience while dreaming! I guess: when the landlord slumbers fine and sweet, his servants will soon notice. They are right goblins and begin doing all kinds of nonsense. There is turmoil, and since the Lord cannot intervene, it sometimes gets a real turmoil. As for example in my following dream.

Still another trip, tonight. I drag the trolley luggage somewhere through a small old town, is it Tübingen, or maybe L'Aquila? In front of me is a row of pretty old houses, with a church skillfully installed. So L'Aquila? But my car had a breakdown, and can only be checked tomorrow morning and maybe repaired. Where should I stay? Two students come by and animatedly talk to each other, apparently about Gerhard Steiff.

"You have to pronounce say everything very clearly, so he wants it."
I ask if they know of a night's accommodation. For interns only, they do an internship with Steiff.

"How nice," I mean, still embarrassed.
The suitcase is getting heavier. You have to stretch your arms forward as if for the Roman greeting, then the suitcase rolls a bit. I'll try it. But I have to get up this defaced free staircase. Half of it is bricked up with cobblestones. Really

Swabian, so pitiful it does look. Finally, I get into a building and a hall. Some people are scattered around. You can look outside through a window into a park with sculptures. The people in here move so slowly as if they would practice something. I see Mr. Dahmen from biocybernetics. It seems like he's trying to look similar to the equestrian statue out there. He looks like Abraham anyway, who in turn almost looks like God. When I ask for accommodation, I get asked back:

"Are you doing an internship with Stalin or Beethoven?"

The blow almost hits me when I consider that. But my cat has jumped on the bed, nothing has happened to me. The animal obviously feels that I should wake up now. No internship, no broken car, comes to my mind immediately. It's time for cat food. Yes, I'm safely back in bed. It remains only a bit of a headache for two days from my bang. In an emergency, the medical expression for this is more of a stroke. May it be so harmless for everyone.

So for explanation: I have not seen Mr. Dahmen for a long time. Most recently, when I had to leave Tübingen and he intended to buy my used car—an Audi. Many years later, on the trip from Heidelberg to Jena, I was again in Tübingen, only for a few hours. KPH, my employer and doctoral supervisor, bought a gift for Tilman while walking through the old town and gave it to me. He bought it in the small shop of Ursula Dahmen in the downtown Tübingen. KPH and I still knew Ursula as Ursula an der Heiden. Uwe an der Heiden had been my colleague; I can confirm that he looks optimistic and serious, but not like Abraham. The latter may have been important for Ursula. You don't know that details anyway.

Without much to be interpreted, one can see from the above lines that the Tübingen years were the happiest in my life. The work and relationship with KPH were decisive for this. On top of that, musical activities. I also knew Ursula and Mr. Dahmen through their joint participation in the university choir under Alexandro Sumski. After a few years, I turned my back on

Sumski. Over time, the constant tension between aspiration and reality was more than annoying and sometimes even ridiculous under Sumski. I was able to join Gerhard Steiff's chamber choir. He became my second caregiver in Tübingen. Miraculously, almost without other external circumstances, all participants felt more balanced under Steiff.

I.2.4   How To Choose a Present,—Thoughts, but No Advice

When I returned home during my study years in the semester break, I always felt like telling in detail what I had learned and what else was new and important to me. But my parents at home were not interested in it. They just wanted to have their well-known son with them for a few days or weeks. About whatever I wanted to ponder, soon I realized that there was little or no interest in it.

What I write so spontaneously here and today has its origin in a similar conflict. Gifts express joy and gratitude, and at the same time, they trigger countless ulterior motives. Therefore I have already written to a classmate: if so, I would rather present a gift in between when I have time to find something interesting. The pressure of expectation at Christmas and birthdays inhibits me.

What did the three wise men from the East bring to the baby Jesus? Incense, myrrh, perhaps cookies etc., indeed irrelevant luxury goods. Shouldn't anyone complain when something like this is still given away for Christmas today. What could they have brought? Perhaps the Gilgamesh epic, and an interesting Babylonic clay table on trigonometry. But even that suggestion seems to me somewhat petty. Because whoever gives his heart or life for others, or is simply there for others, gives much more. Everyone knows that, no matter how well he can contribute himself socially or what his attitude is. But therefore the inhibition to give presents. Probably this is the cause why (almost) all gifts seem so inappropriate.

Finally, I would like to come to examples from my own experience. My doctoral supervisor KPH tells on my last, indeed rare visit, that his wife gave him the book Gödel, Escher, Bach.—

"Yes, should I now begin research on cellular automata." Because that is the topic developed in the book through popular science, brought into multiple relations to the title. KPH is still active in scientific life. Whenever a topic grabs him, he is always in the middle of action, an real participant. If not write a publication, why should one read about it at all. It is only distraction, and being uninvolved embarrasses him. So well, I think, I know my doctoral supervisor. Now he tells me: next time my wife gave a book of my own choice. As a gift, he bought a textbook on molecular biology. How molecules can dissect each other is almost inconceivable. In the end, everything living remains a miracle. So far, so good. I am sitting next to him in the car, and he takes me to Tübingen train station. I don't want to make clumsy comments. But the thought arises back in my mind. Two people who are so important for me and helped me so much. They are now multiple grandparents. Isn't there a better way for such people?

Hilbert got on his seventeenth birthday as a present the mathematical annals tied in leather. (See the excellent biography of Hilbert by Constanze Reid.) He was already so seriously ill with pernicious anemia that a nurse was constantly needed at home. He could no longer consider doing any mathematical work. The volumes of the annals, all bound in leather, were immediately sold by Hilberts.

A counterexample: I really enjoyed the book titled *Clara Schumann, Piano* by Dieter Kuhn. Historically accurate. Giving justice to Robert Schumann, no feminist extremes like in Eva Weissweiler's book. Here is an episode from the book. When Robert Schumann collapsed in his last year, it was probably not clear to any of the dependents whether Schumann had syphilis and which his complaints and symptoms were caused by manic depressive disposition. Johannes Brahms was probably the only one who visited him in the mental hospital. His wife Clara never visited him. Brahms brought Schumann a large world atlas, and Robert made long world trips pointing his fingers.

Now I would like to tell you a little more, which topics have been impressing myself lately. Robert Musil is a writer, not enough recognized, in my opinion. From his youth work, *The Confusions of the pupil Törleß* has been made a movie, unfortunately only in black and white. I got to know Schlöndorff's movie through Hans-Peter. I was not only fascinated and almost haunted by the intolerability of the school, and even more, the boarding school, but also by the upgrowing students (read: pupils) some of whom have a keen interest in mathematics. Nevertheless, only violence against their somewhat dreamy classmate remains in the end. He cannot repay his borrowed money and is tortured. But both happen and become equally credible for the reader through the accuracy with which Musil describes the experience of adolescents. I have never known such literature before.

Musil's main work is *The Man Without Qualities*. The epos is over a thousand pages long. I couldn't read it completely because of my eyes alone. Due to the possibilities of the internet, I also looked for audio books about it. I found two audio versions, as I may have mentioned earlier. A short extract from this is also on my website. In the meantime, Wolfram Berger's reading, in the wonderful Austrian accent, has already been sold out. I only found the first part and just acquired it affordable. So can I give away some of the titles mentioned above? To my sons? It would distract them too much from their work. To whom else? I continue to hesitate.

So all these questions remain open: How far should one guess the needs of the recipient when choosing a gift. How far can a gift show that and how one wants to influence a person. How far can you take *your own* skills and knowledge and interests as hints? It is enough that a few words have been written here and these questions have been asked. Many questions, no answer. Or better: think about it for homework.

I.3 Back to School

I.3.1 The Invitation

Thanks to the diligence of Richard , everybody from our class who wants it may meet in Sulzburg next June. He invites us:

My dear Ones,

I like to hear that—your decision to come to Sulzburg. And Michael will be with us, too. Concerning the accommodations: Rebstock and Dormitorium are centrally located and only 50 m apart from each other (flat route!). Dinner can be taken at the restaurant of the *Rebstock*, they have a separate room, similarly the breakfast. But we may also have breakfast with me at home, no problem. The *Waldhotel* is located three kilometers outside the town, very beautiful, has enough space for all of us, but is not exactly inexpensive. Decide by yourself!

Concerning the program, I have not yet given myself detailed thoughts, because for me at our age more than ever applies Matthew 6,V 34. Here is bible verse quoted:

So don't worry about tomorrow, because tomorrow will take care of itself! Every day has enough with its own plague!

But a tour of our old Ottonian church (more than a thousand years old) and our former synagogue is clearly possible. Moreover, your thematic suggestion, dear Moni, is appropriate and helps to free oneself from indulging in times past.

---Kind regards

Moni is happy to write:

I imagine the program to be similar to last time. Coffee, tour around downtown Sulzburg, dinner with open end. A topic for conversation could be:

"What would I do differently in my life if I came fresh from school again."

That could open up interesting discussions. You see: I pondered about it a little more. Iris has her surgery today. Think about her! Maybe she already has it behind herself and is just waking up gradually.

I.3.2 Who Talks so Lovely about Me

One thing is clear to me,
Franzel is a child prodigy!
He can do math, chemistry and physics,
but he never would get Latin tricks.
Also, in English and in French
it doesn't always work in his bench.
And about German, I hardly dare to speak,
there Franzel is quite weak.
But his eyes soon get brighter
playing a flute piece is lighter.
Because he is a musician keen,
as everyone has heard and seen.

—from the pupil's journal

Already in the old pupil's journal, you had flattered my conviction of being a little genius. Thank you for these pats. But everyone has noticed that it didn't always work properly for me, so I don't really need to repeat it. I still cannot offer a blossom pure success story, only something more like a beer newspaper, in the old tradition. After choosing the mathematical sciences for my profession, voluntarily or not, I got around quite a bit. And it didn't work with a permanent position for a long time.

Finally, I reached a professorship in the USA, more precisely Charlotte in North Carolina; just two years before all the real geniuses, plagued and hungry, come from Russia and China to the USA and especially North Carolina and look for a job there, too.

But let me tell one after another. After studying in Karlsruhe and Zürich and a rather long assistantship at the university of Tübingen, I became visiting professor in Chapel Hill, North Carolina for a year; then three years I was working at the Bundeswehr University in Munich. Right from the start, I had the pleasure of being made a savior in need by seasoned officers. This happened because one of the professors had just dropped more than eighty percent of the students in the intermediate diploma in mathematics. Hence, their superiors rightly worried about the future of the young officers. After three trimesters, the boys thanked me for my lecture. And the dean wrote me a Thank-You letter, which since then I have been happy to enclose my application documents. But unfortunately none of these tricks helped me to become a professor in Germany. I rejected a time position that I could have gained in Dortmund two weeks before moving to the USA. I have been an associate professor at the University of North Carolina at Charlotte since 1989.

Because of all the many moves, my wife and I have renovated two apartments and three houses and created eight new gardens during the past 15 years. I could sing a long song about the work. My wife and me and my two sons Tilman and Dietrich didn't like the many moves. After four years in Charlotte, my family preferred to return to Germany in the end. There were several reasons. I still hadn't got a permanent position, but my wife's time to leave her job could not be extended any longer. We both wanted to send our children to school in Germany, and were just homesick, to tell the truth. So I have now become a hiker between the USA and Germany, more precisely Charlotte and Celle.

At the university in Charlotte, my colleagues are all quite

easygoing. Concerning research, I now have published approximately 30 publications. As far as teaching is concerned, I can honestly say that I like to give lectures. But the lessons are thought to be much more school-like than I actually expected or wanted. The grades are always so terribly important.

But when I say "notes" I prefer to think about music. Already in the pupil's journal, it was so nicely written about me: "But his eyes get brighter, when he even plays a flute piece." Fortunately, nothing has changed for that matter. I regularly play music with a former professor of piano, Thomas Turner. I also practice piano music on my own grand piano. The pieces of music that please me, and are appropriate, become more and more demanding over the years. And my son Dietrich also participates with his cello. I like to accompany him, hopefully carefully and delicately enough.

I.3.3 The Not so Good Old Days

The memory embellishes all our past experiences, as already the Old Greeks did know.

"And if you don't want to listen to the songs from the old westerns, you can go to bed quietly and tomorrow morning drive the pigs out to the fields." You can already read this or something similar in Homer's Illyias.

During my school years, my classmate Kulik had the habit to entertain me with difficult problems from mathematics. In the earlier years, it was a geometric derivation of the binomial formula or the Pythagorean theorem, so later the determination of the focal length of a perspective drawing or a complicated special case to calculate an integral. Too, he was fond of fundamental questions, such as whether the coordinates were the parts of a point. As long as the teacher's directive was not yet in the room, no other classmate dared to think so far ahead.

On the ten-minute walk to the sports field, he keeps asking about my father's career. Now I just got another miserable grade on my German essay. For distraction, I talk about my mother. It was almost her advice for my grief. During her school career, she had got the habit to write *two* class essays during one lesson: during the same hour about two different topics with two different hand writings into two different booklets. First for a friend in her notebook, then the second essay in her own booklet. Later she became an actress. Kulik, too, finds all of this quite interesting.

Next time, on the way to the sports field, he talks about Stalin's hard upbringing with the Jesuits. The sports lessons are a repeated annoyance to me anyway, and my desire to do something more important arises. If not like Stalin, then what else? A week later he catches me in front of the entrance to the locker room. He needs help with the upcoming math exam. Just a piece of paper with the solution handed into the bank behind me, where Kulik is sitting next to Richard,—it would help. Kulik is completely underestimated by the English teacher, which language he speaks fluently, and nevertheless wrongly receives bad grades. Richard has repeatedly told me how Kulik gets stomach cramps before the math exams. For me, it looks like the perfect opportunity to make the world a little more just. Everything happens as agreed upon. Already during the class work, Richard whispers to Kulik .

"The result on Franz's note is wrong."
But Kulik believes my note more than his neighbor's hint. When the class work is returned, Lina shouts at me:

"Rother, I ask for an answer." (She always called me "Rother".)
I have to confess that I wanted to help Kulik.

Wittich approaches me after the hour.

"You should be aware of this: in the *Dritte Reich* you would be rid of your high school diploma."
A few days later, Kulik's school desk is empty. However, nothing happens on the part of the teachers. There is the rumor that he is with his uncle in London. He doesn't come back to school. A few months later, I did visit him with his uncle in London.

Wittich was my only classmate (but possibly not a female comrade) able to accurate judgments already in early childhood. Here is an example. The history teacher had just once again dutifully praised democracy in the Federal Republic of Germany as being perfect, like in heaven.

"In our state, the people determine the government through free elections."

Wittich objects. "I don't see anything like democracy."

"Why?" the teacher wants to know.

"I believe the government in Germany is acting according to the directives from the Americans."

Teacher Leßle agrees fairly loudly. "It is like that anyway, no doubt it is so in the end ..." and the teacher tries to leave the impression that democracy still prevails.

Wittich also told me after the high school exams.

"That you are always the best one will be over quickly during your math studies, as you hopefully do realize."

Only he didn't say that the close community would be over, too.

I.3.4   School Traumata

Some people have dreams like that for a lifetime: they have to pass the exams for the high school diploma once more, again and again. For my part, I was degraded several times, too, when only in a dream. In the beginning, it was still voluntary, for example, to improve my English knowledge,—but only initially. One day, sooner or later, the teacher says,

"Rothe, you're actually quite right here."

Does this happen only to me? Truly not, if one believes the incidents inspired by famous artists and subsequently somewhat adapted and alienated.

Once more, a school bell is ringing.

The new one sits on the bench that the school servant has just carried into the classroom.

"Ton nom?" the French teacher sounds.

He gets up, his hat falls down to the floor. He is close to crying, and can only stammer with fright. When asked about his name for the first and second time, he only produces unidentifiable clams. Only at the third request does he pump up his lungs and tosses out with full strength:

"Charlbovary"

like a "Sharl" with a complicated rat tail, so to speak. Howling roar and laughter. Everyone mimics him.

"Quiet the class, and until tomorrow you will write fifty times: 'Ridiculus sum' ".

At this moment the whole class, from the foremost to the rearmost bench, believes that the new one is ridiculous. What should he ever achieve in life? Yes, the reader will get well informed about it in the following world famous pages. His first wife, who had long since passed away, wanted "just a little more love." And she is financially completely ruined, according to the famous story. Is this dreadful end at least a warning to him for the future? Not at all, the knowledgeable reader knows more precisely.

Another school bell is ringing.

But I want to tell you something about my own school time. In this lecture, our old dear math teacher Lina is covering the quadratic functions. She interrogates the entire class:

"And if you now calculate y equal to x-square,—one after the other for x = 1, 2, ... and so on?"

Richard immediately comes up with a brilliant answer. Well, but Lina continues to drill.

"What are the increases between these numbers?"

He hesitates. Fortunately, Nikolaus helps out. But Lina can't let her darling lie on the left so forgotten. So she asks:

"Now Sündno , explain how the sequence of numbers is continuing."

Richard is not embarrassed. He knows it and Lina is enraptured.

Her enthusiasm rises to the limit. She calls into the class:

"The Sündno has discovered *the law*."

At this moment the whole class, from the first to the last bench, believes that the Sündno discovered *the law*. He is certain to get a place among the immortals, perhaps even in heaven.

Another school bell is ringing.

The opera on Sunday evening was wonderful. But now it's Monday morning, B. hasn't prepared anything. The damned alarm clock rattles. A terrible day. B. is late. Lina or a related monster is already guarding the school entrance. He has to go around the house but does not escape her pursuit and curses at the back entrance, either.

The first hour passes so so. But now it's Latin's turn. Heberdinger was not as long at the hairdresser's last night as B. was in the theater. He was able to sleep in, and can now translate quite rightly and properly. The crammer gets bored.

"Buddenbrook, you are also welcome. You have practiced your Chopeng enough on the bench. So, Mr. Buddenbrook?"

B. rises laboriously and begins to stutter.

"Aurea prima est, ... secundum nullum..."—

"Yes, it doesn't go on? "—" well I'm waiting a little longer." Kulik holds out the book for him. Word after word, he stutters toughly, tears in his eyes. The crammer chases the monkey:

"You have learned? Maybe, *you* believe that. But what have you done? You have drawn immortal verses into the dust. What should become of you?"

At this moment, the whole class, from the foremost to the back row, is convinced that B. has drawn immortal verses into the dust, and does not know what should become of him.

Another school bell is ringing.

In the next math lecture hour, Jäck just sketched another quadratic function nicely onto the board. He may sit down.

"Sündno come to the board and calculate the maximum."

Sündno comes, differentiates, sets the derivative y-prime to zero, and calculates x. A mature achievement, one could say even worthy to Caesar. But Lina is still not saturated in her boring urge to know. She continues to interrogate, like complaining.

"Yes Sündno why is that the maximum now?"
Sündno is an honest and open person and says:

"I'll see that right away."

"Sündno you are a bullhead."

At this moment, the whole class, from the foremost to the back row, is convinced that Sündno is a bullhead. Well, maybe in the end someone else discovered the law, I think. But no such thing does ever happen. And Sündno is a bullhead? The conviction overpowers me, too.

Another school bell is ringing.

During the break, Kulik asks:

"Did you get what Lina explained in the last hour?"
Törleß answers:

"She thinks that if you can't calculate the third roots in the formula, they will become complex. But at the end of the whole calculation, the formula correctly gives the three roots of the third degree equation."

Kulik: "The Lina says, Bombelli or such an Italian has discovered it."

"Yes, yes; I know everything you say. But isn't there something very special about the matter? How should I express that? Just think of it like this: In the beginning, such a calculation contains very solid numbers that can represent meters or weights or anything else tangible, and are at least real numbers. At the end of the calculation, a similar situation holds again. But the beginning and the end are connected by something that doesn't exist. Isn't that like a bridge, of which there are only the first and last pillars and which you still cross as safely as if it were completely there? For me, such a calculation has something dizzy; as if it were a part of the way God knows where to go. The really uncanny thing for me is the strength that lays inside such a calculation, and holds you so tight that you end up properly again."

Beineberg grinned: "You almost speak like our priest: '... you see an apple,—these are the vibrations of light and the eye and so on,—and you stretch out your hand, to steal it— these are the muscles and nerves that set them in motion.—But there is something between the two and brings one out of the other." "And that is the immortal soul that has sinned ..." He imitated the catechist in the way he used to produce the parable.

"Yes, yes, none of your actions can be explained without the soul that plays on you like on the keys of a piano."
Then B. closed dryly: "By the way, I am not very interested in this whole story."

The knowledgeable listener knows how bad was Törleß fate. But in the end, he won't lose all sympathy. After having over- come the events of his youth, he later became a young man of a very fine and sensitive spirit. The past humiliation was that small amount of poison that is necessary to take the overly safe and calmed health of the soul and to give it a finer, sharper, understanding vigilance.

Another school bell is ringing.

But school itself never ends. Pfeiffer is still at school, too. He has to catch up with the high school, they have agreed, even if only for fun. On his first day, when asked, he gets up and says his name with a friendly smile.
"With one or two f?"
"With three."
"Why with three?"—
"With however many, Pfeiffer, you will have to get used to discipline."
At this moment nobody in the class, from the first to the last bench, knows with how many f's the name P?eif??fer is written.

The discipline is bad. Teachers are missing from the empire. Minister Rust banned the film because "he ridicules the school."

Heinz Rühmann is alarmed and travels to the east. His aviator friend Oberst Angermund negociated for him. After a long-hour train journey, he is now within a triple ring of barbed wire. He is waiting. Those responsible prefer to watch the film by themselves. He reads a bit in the library. Afterwards, while walking, he discovers behind another barbed wire fence a small bent man, and next to him a German shepherd dog who follows and adapts to his steps. A few days later, Rühmann can hardly believe what he had experienced. From that day on everyone in the cinema can learn that Pfeiffer is written with three f's, one in front of the egg, and two behind the egg. And Heinz Rühmann smiles on the canvas.

The last school bell is ringing.

Dear friends: just consider this an end. All books that have inspired these lines are— or should have been banned once upon a time. How can my humble lines change anything about it? But they shouldn't prevent you from having the beer be tasty for you tonight.

I.4   Natural Philosophy

I.4.1   You Cannot Swim in the Same River Twice

I Ponder

What would I do differently in my life if I came fresh from school again? I've been asking myself that a lot more often than I would like to admit. But be honest: from a time distance, the life of those past days looks so beautiful and easy. Wouldn't you have left so many opportunities unused? Wouldn't a little more diligence and effort have been appropriate? I've always been an "occasionally quite hardworking" (but) seasonal worker. But with so much more diligence, wouldn't I have died of a severe heart stroke soon? Yes, everything could have been different. Life is a chain of annoying little instances and coincidences. Looking back always produces a very different appearance than the rare look ahead. Because of all of this, such considerations are all too quickly only a waste of time.

And yet, I think it makes sense to ask the question about one's own past for an hour every few weeks. If, for example, I notice something that is so important to me and has ever happened to me repeatedly, then it happens that I want to talk to my children about it, and to be able to give advice. In this restricted case, thinking may make sense. In this context, I notice how badly I have always dealt with my financial affairs.

The Philosopher Speaks

Before I fall completely quiet, a few literature references help. In his main work *The Man Without Qualities*, Musil emphasizes: "Everything could have developed differently." Like me, he sees the world's course as a chain of random events. In his biographical sketches, Friedrich Dürrenmatt emphasizes how life has for him always been a labyrinth: during early childhood while playing in grain fields and grain storages, and later on in the arcades and alleys of downtown Bern.

Only those who want may follow my further philosophizing about science. At least in this labyrinthine world, there exist all degrees of the likely and unlikely. This is obvious for the realm of elementary particles. Can there be a journey back in time? There are important objections to this possibility, as follows: as experience is happening for the second time, my time-traveled person would become doubled. Then an automatism begins and with every repetition of life which in the course must take place automatically, additional even smarter copies of myself participate in the additional journey through life. In exponential growth, a super-person is created. The effect is similar to the well-known acoustic feedback. This super-person would automatically become smarter and more and more skillful and therefore more successful until this army of clones would subdue and devastate the entire world, and ultimately destroy itself. I claim that the existing labyrinth of world events is only possible grace of the arrow of time pointing towards the future, and with the help of random events.

Shortly After the Big Bang

Here is still another speculation. The arrow of time directed towards the future, I imagine, arose after the Big Bang in a short time, during which the excessive gravity initially still allowed time travel into the past. But these instances were quickly destroyed again by the constantly increasing feedback. This indicates a mechanism, by which may be created a globally valid cosmological time. Only *after* that initial stage, random events and natural law can work together and continuously build the world, see "cosmic inflation" stimulated by Stephen Hawking, among others, and "the first three minutes" by Steven Weinberg. With the combination of atoms, the charged world broth becomes transparent, and the starry sky appears. And every new part is realized as a single one of many possibilities and becomes irrevocable for a later course. Many greater spirits have all of these ideas put together in small steps, and some speculation may have already been considered. But scientific tact and caution naturally require speculation not to be shot in the herb as I do with my suggestions here. In the end, it is better if the philosopher is silent.

Leave the Church in the Village

During the thoughts above, I have related the question of what I would do differently in a second life only to myself personally. Next I let myself be drawn into daring cosmological speculations. The following idea remains with me as the most obvious consequence:

It is principally impossible to repeat the course of world events or a part of them.

"You can't get into the same river twice",

an aphorism attributed to Heraclitus. Nevertheless, it is the general basis of the law and at least almost everyone is convinced that one should be accountable, and one has to think about how to act and what is to be avoided.

I.4.2   Time Travel

But now I turn to the much more interesting and profound self-references in physics. The speculative physicist awakens in me. Is time travel possible? Special as well as general relativity proves that time travel to the future *is* indeed possible. The flight around the world is sufficient for a very small journey to the future, as experimentally proven by taking appropriate very accurate clocks with you. In this experiment, one partner flies around the world with the exact clock, while the other partner stays at home with a second such clock. After returning, a comparison of the two clocks shows that the traveler is a bit younger than the one who stayed at home. Incidentally, the poor guy doesn't even have to wait at the airport—he can safely go home to comfort him that he is now a little older than the more daring travel agent. Staying in a strong gravitational field is another way to travel forward in time. One would have to protect oneself from the direct action of the field inside the cavity of a heavy lead ball.

But does there exist a journey back in time? In that case, you could go through your own life again. That gives enough contradictions, see the above. The genial Gödel has found interest in general relativity when he walked together with Einstein to the same *Institute for Advanced Studies* every day. He discovered a mathematically correct solution to the field equations of general relativity, which contains a closed space-time geodesic. As a consequence, staying on this world line brings oneself inevitably into one's own past. Roger Penrose has praised this piece of work as independent and creative. What does the recently deceased Hawking say about that matter? There is a video with him where he talks about time travel, too. He claims that the closed space-time geodesics inevitably lead to a feedback effect, as everyone knows from the use of a microphone that amplifies too loudly. The initial seed of noise necessary for this effect is created by the quantum fluctuations. Again (as with the black hole) the quantum fluctuations have a decisive influence, and are changing everything. No person or measure instrument could survive the radiation prevailing on a closed space-time geodesic. The journey through time is stopped!

So far the mathematical and physical world correspond quite well. When used in mathematical programming, the feedback only leads to constant repetition. A three-line program easy to be produced with the computer language *Pascal* will write and rewrite the word "Pascal" forever. Such a programming code runs in this programming language without any problems—as long as you want or until you switch off the computer. The journey into the future corresponds roughly to the call of a new instance of the same program with a smaller input. This is permissible in programming and is often used when writing recursive programs. Accordingly, the journey through time and into the future is also possible. One's possibilities reach their limit by the limitation of the funds used, so it is only possible to travel forward in time to the near future. On the other hand, the journey into the past roughly corresponds to the call of the same program with greater input. This is not permissible, but leads to programs with loops and infinite runtime. Accordingly, traveling back in time is in principle impossible.

Here is a remark by Klaus Schubert, professor of elementary particle physics.

I continue to fight my way through Lee Smolin's excellent book. I am now in Chapter 15 (Beyond String Theory) of the twenty chapters. Very sympathetic how the principle of causality is made the most fundamental of all principles. According to Smolin's desideratum on page 241, the theory of quantum gravity should follow from three principles:

(1) Space is emergent

(2) its fundamental description is discrete

(3) this description involves causality in a fundamental way

Part II

Important Topics

II.1 About Social Life

II.1.1 Merkel's Surprise

```
Hello friends,
```

Time is running and Christmas is almost there, and soon New Year. After Richard 's serious Christmas sermon, I send a somewhat lightweighted greeting to New Year, with current political references. What about political world events. The devastating mistakes of the past decades make me despair. As soon as Merkel has opened the door to the future of German politics only a gap wide, everything seems possible again. Is the next Chancellor a cleaning lady or a pilot?

```
                    —Kind regards Franz
```

The Candidates

But one after the other. The election of the party leader of the CDU is to be held on December 7. With Angela's help, she has already got prepared: Ms. Annegret Krampp-Karrenbauer is a talented politician, and at the carnival she was not a princess, no, she was a cleaning lady.

From the other side, flying his own small Cessna, he arrived, the multiple chairman of the supervisory board of Blackrock in Germany: Mr. Friedrich Merz. He announces that he is a medium-class millionaire and (perhaps to prove it) gives his tax declaration on a beer mat. At least in this regard, he is economical. He has learned well from Mr. Schäuble, if not from worse ones. The sir looks emphatically fresh. Our so briskly liberal Mr. Lindner can take an example from him. One soon hears of rivalries with Merkel sixteen years ago. Of whom does Mr. Merz remind me? What kind of person is he?

Some Associations from Literature

In my seclusion, I like to use figures from literature as a comparison. Who was similarly rich? Who made use of his money so secretly? In Jane Autin's most well-known work *Pride and Prejudice*, Mr. Darci from Pemberley is a super-rich great gentleman. One only mentions his annual earnings in a whisper. A modest man could endure twenty years from it. But throughout the story, he becomes more and more sympathetic. After the youngest of the five Bennett daughters is kidnapped by villain Wickham and almost ends up in the gutter, Darci manages to save her. As the guardian of his sister, who is ten years younger, he has detailed knowledge of the milieu of the London cheap side and manages to find the kidnapped Lydia there. In skillful negotiations, he uses his own money, among other things, and finally enables Lydia's honorable marriage to her kidnapper Mr. Wickham. Nobody, least of all the clever Elizabeth would have expected him to do all of this. She had rejected his first marriage proposal and beyond that, had made serious allegations against him. The two smartest from th story come together and get married. Darci has a noble core in a rough shell. He can even admit his own mistakes and weaknesses.

Could this be a role model for Friedrich Merz? Here is a counter-draft: after twenty years, Dürrenmatt lets the old lady fly back to her home dump, on her own plane, too. She has now made millions with speculations and sees the time has come for her to settle an old bill. The local car dealer was her lover formerly, he had covered up the affair. She is now being received with brass music, but immediately withdraws to her hotel and waits for everything to come. As a starter, she has promised millions of dollars in donations to her home village of Güllen and its inhabitants. But on one condition: justice. More and more councilors are finding excuses to accuse the car dealer. The village distributes its money even before it has arrived. The evil end is coming, their revenge is successful. After the car dealer is dead, the old lady immediately disappears.

Could that story be a role model for Friedrich Merz? Settle old affairs, his private plane,—to just wait, and provoke the public with daring tales and promises. All of this fits quite well. I don't know which comparison fits better for Mr. Merz, and I probably never shall know.

Everyone was immediately taken in with the fresh neoliberal gentleman. You believe him too: his money and the sweet revenge. But dear Mr. Merz, I ask you, has it not have been told in an even older classic: "The revenge is mine, says the Lord." And this classic even firms on the same feature as your party. How should that be made compatible? Perhaps, Mr. Merz, you simply got into the wrong party. Mr. Lindner is pale with envy seeing your show and your money. It is the most sincere admiration. What is the robbery of a bank against the establishment of a bank?

The Congratulations

Meanwhile, the new general secretary of the CDU has been elected. After my congratulations, I would like to whisper another piece of advice to Annegret: So if unluckily your tax return does not fit on a beer mat, then at least your name should fit on it. Just try it as an "Annegret Cart Builder", in German Annegret Karrenbauer. It sounds really down to earth, doesn't it. With both legs, she firmly stands in life. What is urge and pending in the country, she sees it, rolls up her sleeves, and gets to it. And then I still would like to add: for the fans you are simply AKB. One can see right away that you can say not only A but also B. It's an indicator of a great future, maybe as Chancellor. All the best.

The beer mat has unfortunately been lost. As a weak consolation, only my newspaper still exists. But what kind of a newspaper! But sorry, I have completely lost sight of the old bad youth memories. My nice essay ... again ... the purest beer newspaper! I no longer can hear it, sponge over it. Nevertheless, once more. I wish all dear friends and fellows a successful New Year. Happy New Year!

II.1.2   The Answer from Hans-Peter

Dear Franz,

Thanks for considering the current political situation in Germany, and in particular of the CDU. If you look at the current state of the world, it is clear that trumpism is a hit now everywhere (that is, a "symptom"); not always in the realisation of an asshole like Donald Pussy-Tr..., —nevertheless ...see Turkey, Russia, Indonesia, Poland, Hungary, and so on, and so on. So why should that just stay away from Germany? We have a new CDU woman from the far west of Germany, which is ultra-catholic, and on the right overtakes the current pope. Last time, it was an unbeliever from the extreme east, without children, so quite acceptable for a third of the German population.

Now it's about moving to the right
and (appearing as) "Christian"—

Why did the Horst Seehofer with his "upper limit" (for refugees) eat chalk? Time works for him, as it works for Merz because "the people want a real man", preferably one like Trump, one from "god's own country", a millionaire: because that's the hope of the so-called man from the street: if "HE" does it, I can do it, too!

Which has to say: the one on stage in front, a chancellor (or a president) should hand out the lost millions—the others have cheated on me, have betrayed me on my life's work! All those, the lying press, the system politicians, the eastern or western elite! What Eastern Germany had wanted, together with what Western Germany wants: in the FRG like the GDR, everybody has a job as in the east (no matter what you do) and everybody is rich—like it used to be in the west.

But the matter has a catch: not even capitalism as analyzed by Marx would work in this way! (But who still knows Marx?) So in the end: a "strong man" should bring what Kohl once promised us: blooming landscapes without end. Merz therefore still has his time ahead of him, even if it is a time that is passée. People are just a pack—in earlier times and now even more so in the age of the internet. If you have read a little in Nietzsche's "Untimely Considerations", part 2, you will have noticed that the backwards-oriented contemplators of history always wanted to have back the "good old days"—those which never had existed.

Specifically: Merkel will give up her job next year, the election will take place between the extreme right (AFD) and the CDU/CSU; the latter will need coalition partners. The available ones are the AFD, the green party (the new religious party of the forgiveness trade: I drive my mobile home and travel on vacation x times by plane or luxury steamer, and elect "green" for compensation), and finally the FDP. Who will make the run?

The situation in France is similar, with the difference that Marcon has not a party at his rear, but a movement "to the front"— So we live in a society of desiring—it is always Christmas, and the Christmas man we choose should do it. (Amazon will deliver.) The French are just going to do it:

(1) Macron gave in to the pressure of the street, so let's stop.

(2) Macron gave in to the pressure of the street, so let's go on.

Who is right? I bet, it will be the collapse soloists. Welcome to the "brave new world". —lghp

II.1.3 About Ernst Bloch

First I have heard from Ernst Bloch from my friend Thomas Reghely, who studied philosophy in Tübingen and with whom I shared the apartment. He was always so enthusiastic about

Bloch and often asked: when will we have a real demo again? But it helped me more that he always warned me to keep the fridge clean. In the meantime, he may have become a tax advisor in Frankfurt. Later I read Ernst Bloch's *The Principle of Hope* during long train journeys. I was amazed at how entertaining these three volumes are. Unfortunately, I have never found them as audio books. Bloch's speeches are partly available as an audiobook, but I don't remember half a sentence of them. During the Weimar time, Bloch was probably mainly a journalist. He had to flee the Nazis and wrote the "The Principle of Hope" in American exile. In the USA, however, he was badly received, too. After the Second World War, he became a professor in Leipzig, but fled to Tübingen after the Hungarian uprising. Fame and success came over him after having three times to escape! His main theme is the utopias through human history, in addition to Marx also Thomas Münster and *The Sun State* by Thomas Morus. He literally conjures up the future and hope. He sees the whole culture and civilization from this point of view. For my taste, however, it is usually too abstractly philosophical, unfortunately.

II.1.4　The Lemming University

The University of Cologne was awarded to be an excellence university. At the same time, there are not enough teachers for freshmen lectures. Some time ago, the journal *Spiegel* showed a picture of a lecture for frechmen in a large amphitheater auditorium with over a thousand listeners. The curriculum urgently needs to be redesigned. I know it from my own experiences, and even more from the failures of my sons. The incentive and charm of theoretical science are enormous. Only someone who has no interest in theory anyway, like my younger offspring, remains unimpressed. On the contrary, all applications are full of dirty ambiguities.

Almost every other student is from the beginning more and

more drawn to abstraction, and in the end much too much. They suffer the adverse consequences very soon, at the latest when starting their professional career. The free economy evidently requires any physicist or mathematician to learn quickly. All of this may be possible for a few geniuses, but each academic one level below will only have been assigned a too small task for too long, or will be completely shipwrecked. In addition: the age at which academics marry gets later and later. This is very unhealthy, and not only for women. It is almost biblical evidence that old fathers are cruel and bad for their children.

The problems cannot be solved by the young generation alone. Germany, France, Switzerland, Holland, indeed most European countries, would have to set up at least one university with the clear goal of advancing from the very beginning of the studies the technologies that will be decisive in the future and aligning the course with this requirement from the outset. The topics lie on the street, I just pick out:

- Large-scale hydraulic engineering,

- Sea water desalination,

- large-scale production of alternative fuels.

- Furthermore operations research, mathematically sound logistics and management, etc.

The little economic gain from the CO_2 levy could finally be used sensibly. When I think about the future like this, I realize how badly our Chancellor is failing and leaving everything in bad shape.

Dear Franz,

thanks for your lemming letter, which is me for a comment on Frankfurt and Thomas Reghely: T.R. started a philosophical working group around the corner years ago. Indeed, one of my former high school graduates was also from the party. In the meantime I see T.R. regularly from a distance in the Katarinen church at the organ concerts on Mondays and Thursdays: it is funny how small the world is when you know how to take a closer look.

—Hans-Peter

II.1.5 No American

By the way, I do not want to become an American citizen,— in my case, there is no need for it. In this respect, too, I'm neither Einstein nor Thomas Mann. My son Tilman tells me it is binding American custom that detailed opinions should only be exchanged with like-minded people, especially when these are not completely justified anyway. I think that is wrong, although it is certainly most common practice. See my next mail.

Hello friends,

What Hans-Peter and what I write occasionally, somewhat less, about politics is, in my opinion, of general interest. One has to be happy to be able to communicate with people of different opinions and backgrounds. This is not completely self-evident, as it becomes clear to me when I imagine a similar discourse

(1) with the colleagues in the department in a similar style; or

(2) standing as teacher in front of the class.

In the case (1), in my opinion, the dissemination of the above information would still be permissible today, but would it also be recommended? In the case (2), there are strict rules regarding abstinence from any talk on the sideline. As I think about it, I also realize for people who are comfortably saddled in a permanent position, all of this becomes more delicate. As for me, I think I have always taken enough into account my counterparts here. Just speaking to people of the same opinion is also a sneaky form of censorship.

—All the best. Franz

II.1.6   Hans-Peter and Adult Education

After passing through all forms of left-wing radicalism (Horkheimer, Adorno, Habermas, Walter Benjamin, Marx, Lenin, Stalin, Trotzky, Mao), both in Germany and in France, Hans-Peter had tried again to get a PhD grade. But I gave up already in the 70s because—although I had already completed part of my dissertation—I felt the first beginnings of merciless hate and competition for academic positions. The attitude that every academic is hostile to the next one (and I really mean "enemy" and not just "opponent" or "different"!), did not at all fit to my political and scientific ethics. That is why—like once Wittgenstein—I focused myself on a career at high-schools, in order to offer helpful guidance to young people and young adults, BEFORE they enter the university, or in any case support another life perspective for them. Political science and philosophy and to this day: theater studies as well as especially psychoanalysis have never left me since I started my studies in Heidelberg in 1966. (Gadamer, a student of Heidegger, Karl Loewith, Karl Popper, Wittgenstein, Carl Schmitt, Freud, Lacan, Derrida, Samuel M. Weber and many others)

In the rickety armor of an orphan who was adopted by a proletarian couple and grew up in the narrow social framework of a village in the musty 50s, I was just too poorly equipped for bourgeois life. In any case, this should not be a complaint or a reproach (although the opposite always resonates with all negations), because indeed my adoptive parents have helped me to live a reasonably justifiable life, as good as they could and with huge sacrifices of their own. But I never lost my faith in the maxim

audiatur et altera pars!
Here is the translation:
"The other part is also to be heard."
It is the principle that no one should be convicted without a fair hearing that allows each party to respond to the charges against

them.

Hans-Peter continues to write: Indeed what is called "identity" these days, in reality means "identification"—namely: "identification with the desire of the desire of the other" (genitivus subjectivus and objectivus).
I call it "original predication". It only works based on the mechanism of the LANGUAGE itself, its ability to create substitutions. Every letter, each word only gains meaning and hence "sense" through another letter, through another word in fact through an infinite chain of supplementations. It happens throughout life, yes, one may call it a conversation beyond one's own death: this is perhaps in toto the "law of life", and it dominates living as well as so-called dead, culture as well as nature. I close by citing Hölderlin:

> We are a sign, without interpretation,
> We are painless and almost have
> Lost the language in a foreign land
> *—Hölderlin: Mnemosyne, second version*

Dear Hans-Peter,

As I see, you are convinced that one has to educate the young people before they go to college. It's too late for me to see how right you are. Already your successes tell this. On the spot, I find four books being published that you wrote between 1978 and 1990. During your full-time job as a French teacher, you founded the psychoanalytic working group Frankfurt am Main in 1995. You have been a board member of this society for many years, and you continue to very often write reviews on movies. Last year there was published a book translated from French by yourself.

In light of that, does your above letter not sound like "fishing for compliments?" Your merits were not possible from nowhere by themselves, but only became possible through your intensive continuous education and engagement. In addition, all the communication with our former classmates, to whom I also owe a lot of suggestions.

Kind regards Franz

II.2 Philosophy and Mathematics

II.2.1 Lost with Giorgio Agamben

Giorgio Agamben was an attentive and critical student of Heidegger in the 1960s. He has been working on the "deconstruction" of Western thinking—with the expression of Hans-Peter. Agamben has been teaching in Italy, Germany and the USA, more precisely Chicago, the same university where Jean-Luc Nancy or Sam Weber, has been teaching, too. He is a student of Heidegger and Freud.

Hello Hans-Peter,

Here are a few of my thoughts about Agamben. What is written here, is just a beginning. Maybe you still enjoy it a bit. Because I don't hear from you anymore. I'm somehow not ready with Agamben. I believe that Giorgio Agamben's article addresses both a problem of mathematical logic and a physical problem - but both are mixed even more than one is permitted to. I am a little upset that all developments that have happened since Gottlob Frege are by no means known to and appreciated by Agamben. The danger for great men is always to want too much. After the first stroke of genius, they fail. The popular opinion then often throws away all new knowledge. This remark refers to Frege, Cantor, Hilbert, Gödel, Einstein. Maybe only Feynman and Hawking were a little more careful and conscious about this danger. You can't get any further with such sloppy cutting corners, as it is a popular mistake. I need a little rest now. I'll hang on to what I wrote. Can Agamben be better German or English. Do you have an email address from him?

—All the best and see you soon. Franz

Hans-Peter, thanks for my persistence. However, his reflections are on a completely different level. Currently, he is dealing with the problem of "identity and identification", especially in the psychoanalytic sense. I cannot imagine what to know or say about that matter. Hans-Peter goes on and mentioned to be working with language theory and its conclusions: in that context one will encounter the Möbius band and the Borromean knot at every turn. I can find out what all that is, but why should it cause dizziness and fear? My imagination is of course limited, so too complicated twists can cause dizziness and nausea for me, too. But for what reason should one use differentiable or topological manifolds, and especially the examples for them mentioned above, in the context of models for consciousness processes. There is not even a hint for explanation. Why two-dimensional manifolds, it seems an arbitrary choice for me. As a suitable space describing the color perception, a few three-dimensional manifolds were proposed in a seminar hour at KPH.

A mail address from Agamben would be useful. H.P. writes he unfortunately can no longer find it on his PC. "Welcome to the club," I want to say. Even PC crashes, they have breakdowns, computers are just like people and almost as forgetful. H.P. recommends a search on the internet. That hasn't helped me so far. Dear reader, where did I err, and worse, kidnapped you. Like the early Egyptian ascetics, I will now retreat to my "cave" and deal with my past at the university. Hans-Peter is now dealing with his, and not just his, political past and present, on the occasion of the 50-year celebrations of 1968. Hopefully you may follow him there (to another cave). The Agamben problem is only part of the action among others. The fight continues to rage. Agamben's new book on *Karma* is quite strong tobacco, but is extremely spiritual! Hans-Peter also writes, therefore, the discourse with me is somewhat on the back burner. Despite all the recognition, he does not like to pursue the mathematical approaches in detail. I also tried to protect the reader of this hardness as much as possible.

Together with Hans-Peter, we are still speculating about Georg Cantor, the founder of set theory. Like some of his colleagues from the humanities, H.P. believes in a case of spiritual self-abandonment. Let me in the following make a few remarks about this matter.

Certainly there is a hiatus of many years in Cantor's life, during which he did not and probably could not deal with mathematics. In Cantor's letters from these years, one reads that he has not felt so fresh lately, and among other topics, one finds speculation about the origin of Shakespeare's dramas. In any case, after several years he straightens up again, and published a second proof for the uncountability of the real numbers, and presented this piece of research at the founding meeting of the DMV (German Mathematics Association).
This famous *diagonal argument* is closely related to Russell's paradox. A little later he was familiar with the paradoxes of set theory. According to some biographers, they didn't throw him off track. These biographers say that he would have had psychological problems, too, if he had been simply a baker.

May that be as ever, Hans-Peter points out quite correctly: universal problems are not brought to bear with impunity. I don't know if he had a tangible woman around him, like Hawking, who occasionally reminded him: "Stephen, you are not God." Remaining on firm ground doesn't seem the wrong thing to me.

II.2.2 Consolation with Günther Grass

Not an inmate of a medical or nursing home, still I'm legally blind in both eyes, I can give the evidence in writing. Many people tend to recap their lives now and then. I lack the immense urge to do so. Famous people of all times have always given me more landmarks in my years than my grandparents. So why write? What do I want to achieve?

I love to explain complicated mathematics, but few like to listen to me. I can't catch the attention through small talk. I can hardly keep them as long as they do not see material benefits for themselves. So I always think a little of the benefits of the others. This rather dirty truth has enabled me to teach at a university for a long time.

Even formerly, while still with my full eyesight, at least on the right eye, I aimed at a further goal. A little more clarity in the development of science and especially mathematics would be my goal. Where to start? I don't have a tin drum, and if exercise sheets are something similar, I had to say goodbye and farewell because of my bad eyes. Too, exercises have to fit the daily needs. Only the computer remains for me, with easy typing and good memory. I am only too often confused by the need to tidy up the notes every now and then, clearing the way by specifying titles and topics. But too often I lose interest in making lists. Or can no longer find your own old notes.

All of this awakens bad memories beginning already back in school. Is it not written already in the Bible: the mind stirs up wherever it wants. The gentleman who was my German teacher didn't want to know about that. And teases us to begin our essays by laying out a table of contents. What did he really want? I am sure he wanted to do his doctorate in Egyptology, already a long time ago during the war, and he was eager to see and learn more and more from ancient Egypt. One day, after a long expertise talk about the ancient Egypt it really slipped out of him:

"While visiting Kairo the next time, we may perhaps spare an hour and go to the Islamic Museum, too."
Today, when recalling that moment, I think: perhaps there is no other way to see today the Egyptian exhibition because this is the only way to get tickets to Kairo's Egyptian museums. How times have changed!

The museums all have a natural inclination towards order. But mathematics has so much order in itself that you prefer to let your thoughts wander when you invent and search. Where does one speak of the infinite in any scientific discipline? Only in mathematics. But unlike anything imaginable talking and pondering about God, one does not deal with faith. What is there as a barrier to the unknown and unknowable, is it not more and nothing else than the current customs of thinking people, their efforts to bring the sum of the knowledge into today's usual form. But these issues are specific to the present time, too. At least in this context, it becomes clear that every science should have and value its history. How late did I learn to appreciate the above told! From all of the above, one somehow hopes for more knowledge and more truth. Also, useful new insights and just progress. Some of you have heard of this in one form or another. What does this mean for myself. Life and years passing by make oneself more humble. However, for me still has remained the hope of clarifying some of the topics from mathematics, on which I have worked to some extend at least. I definitely like clarity much better than order. How do I gain more clarity?

"The surface must remain rough. Something unfinished should not pretend to be finished."
The smart reader may have noticed from whom I'm trying to learn here.

How do I gain more clarity? All knowledge begins, so to speak, in the middle: where the world of everyday life touches science. From there you go backwards, towards better clarification of more and more basics and contexts, and forward to new conclusions, examples, and surprises. Seen in this way, it is not just Günther Grass' mood to start a story in the middle. The middle is the part closest to everyday life. Hence by starting in the middle one has reached the old didactic principle "from the simple to the advanced".

On the other hand, it is ultimately modern to shatter the classical forms, to free yourself from the constraints of time and space, as my dear Günther Grass justifies. I have a soft smile because I still want to do my own efforts to free me from the constraints of time and space.

My geometry students probably didn't mind if my course

started with Thales and his right angle in a semicircle, or sometimes with the proportions. I often started with Cantor's idea for the introduction to discrete mathematics:

"A set is a gathering of objects of our thinking or our imagination into a whole."

This sentence sounds so harmlessly nice and easy to understand. It leads to the paradise-like infinities too quickly. With or without paradoxes it soon becomes obvious that well-defined terms are needed.

So it is better to speak from the very beginning about a *set* and its *elements*, and to introduce the relation "Element lies in the set" at the beginning—written as a formula:

"x is the element of A." or simply $x \in A$.

I didn't find this relation—"is an element of"—in Cantor's view of set theory. It probably goes back to Bolzano, or to Zermelo. Gradually, it may also dawn on the reader that *well-defined terms* are requiring more than simply generally understandable language. Additionally, these terms should and must be clearly exemplified. The first steps in the foundations of mathematics, i.e. the basic concepts in logic, set theory, and algorithms form the first part of Hilbert's program, and these are common knowledge for the modern mathematicians of today. I say and write: *these basic concepts have become commonplace.* Therefore, the first part of Hilbert's program is a major step forward. The mathematician Nelson, in a recent review of the history of foundations of mathematics, even speaks of a further progressive step of the enlightenment.

II.2.3 Sirs, It Has Been My Pleasure, You Excuse Me

Some time ago, approximately 25 years, it really happened to me like that. In the past December, Putin had been voted the *Person of the Year* by the *Times* magazine. The following

January, the reporters from Times wrote an article about their invitation to Putin in Moscow. A few weeks after having read the article in the Times, I was just going to hold my geometry lesson again. I was talking about the lunes of Hippocrates. These are some very specially shaped areas that are delimited by a few circular arcs, which have the peculiarity that they can be constructed by compass and straightedge. Additionally, a square of equal area can be constructed in this manner, too.

The first of these lunes were discovered by Hippocrates in Ancient Greece. Hippocrates was one of the first after Thales and Pythagoras to discover new topics in mathematics and especially geometry, and he was probably the first to teach mathematics with the purpose to make money. The subject is historically interesting because the evidence of exact mathematical proof has been handed down here long before the imperialist Euclid wrote his *Elements*.

"Yes, dear students, this was the starter now, the difficult part is to rigorously prove that all cases have been found for such lunes. Some Russian mathematicians succeeded to give this proof only in the 1950s.

And now I'm doing something very much similar to president Putin, and since we're already talking about Russia, may I now tell you: Gentlemen, the light starter has certainly put you in a youthful mood. But I don't want to torture you with the less digestible material which should follow. So I was very happy that you from the "Times" thought of me as the "person of the year" , and now excuse myself." P. gets up and releases the reporters from the *Times* before the main dish can be served.

"Yes, dear students, and so I will do it with you now, so as not to spoil your youthful courage and the joy of geometry." In this manner or similarly talked the former professor Rothe (please pronounce it as impossible as the Americans do!), just for entertainment before he was moving on to the agenda, i.e. grades, material for the next test, etc.

But the horrific, obscure, and terrifying thing, after all, is this: Neither I nor anyone else had become suspicious about P. by this incident.— For my part, it was nothing but, as intended, a little breather. And whether it was more than a slight embarrassment for the journalists from *Times*,— I doubt by now.

P.S. Yesterday I heard from Markus Lanz that the attack on a theater in Moscow allegedly committed by Chechens the year before had been staged by P., too. Just with the purpose that he may start the second Chechen war, with area bombings of the city of Grozny. (Was that only after P. was appointed person of the year?)

II.3   Kafka

II.3.1   Reading Kafka's Story *A Country Doctor*

Hello Hans-Peter,

Please try if it works for you. I send you *A Country Doctor* from the CD with Gerd Westphal's Kafka recitation. It's really great. I've listened to it three times lately.

All the best Franz

Dear Franz:

Now concerning Kafka: of course, that's still hype, and I hope you know Kafka's letter to the father! (If not read or hear it immediately!!!) "The country doctor" is a wonderful surrealistic story, in which the black romance of Johann Heinrich Füssli (1741–1825, in England known as Henry Fuseli), even the Moses of Michelangelo ("the fingers in the beard") appear and which, on the other hand, feeds the later vampire films (Polanski's dance of the vampires, etc.). In addition, I realize during my latest reading a fundamental criticism of religion ("the pastor is sitting at home"), but also the criticism of belief in the modern (natural) science ("but the doctor should repair everything") . . . and—last but not least—not to forget: Kafka's fear

of femininity or his own sexual drive (see the servant against
Rosa—). But what interests me most are YOUR own associa-
tions. I think that would be great!

—Lghp

Why does fascinate me in this story? Especially the horses.
They are a healthy sibling pair of spriting browns. Crapping out
of a pigsty, they fly the earthly wagon all over the place. Curious
and cheeky like a cat, both of them put their heads through the
window and even tear it open. They are "sewn together" from
different animal species.

Moreover, the breathless, furious chase during the whole
night and fog campaign, which brings the poor doctor to the
most extreme tension, amidst the incredible surprises. And
in spite of that, everything seems credible and suitable for the
rushed life of a country doctor. In the beginning, it wasn't more
than that.

While reading once more, a lot of observations were added.
The whole story begins to look fishy. Hans-Peter gives a mytho-
logical explanation that I would not have come up with by myself. But I want to point out the discrepancies without following
a so far-fetched interpretation. The common people's doubts
about religion and how their belief is replaced by expectations
in modern medicine. The country doctor finds this attitude non-
sensical or at least exaggerated:

> I am not a world improver and leave him alone. I am
> employed by the district and do my duty to the
> edge, to where it gets almost too much. Poorly
> paid, I'm generous and helpful to the poor.

> That's how are the people around me. Always ask
> the impossible from the doctor. They have lost
> their old faith; the pastor sits at home and tugs
> apart the chasubles, one by one; but the doctor
> should repair everything with his tender surgical
> hands. Well, I do it as you want: I didn't offer

> myself; if you use me for sacred purposes, I will
> let it happen to me; what else do I, an old country
> doctor, want—robbed of my maid?

Ultimately, the music also goes through this whole metamor-
phosis, with a thank-you chorus onto modern medicine. Believe
it or not, something similar exists in an opera by Puccini.

Why does he keep thinking about his maid? Couldn't he
since a long time have taken her as his medical assistant? His
relationship with her seems good and familiar enough for such
a task.

Already when he initially considers the patient to be healthy,
it becomes evident that not everything is in good shape with
the doctor. Soon afterwards, the patient also notices during the
examination:

> My trust in you is very little. You're just shaken off
> from somewhere, don't arrive at your own feet.
> Instead of helping, you narrow my deathbed. I
> would prefer to scratch your eyes off.

And then the doctor is quite satisfied after having explained
to the patient that he must die. One has to admit, in modern
medicine, despite all successes, many things go wrong, too. But
even more, is fishy. I guess, he is more a euthanizer than a
doctor. The doctor sees and tells the patient that he wanted
to hurt himself. In the end, the doctor and the sick both agree
with this view and even find it good.

> I, who have been at so many a bed of the sick, far
> and wide, I tell you: your wound is not so bad.
> Created at an acute angle with two blows from
> the hoe. Many ones offer their side and hardly
> hear the hoe in the forest, let alone that it comes
> closer to them.

> "Is it really as you tell, or are you deceiving me in a
> fever?"

> "It really is like that, take the honorary word of a doctor with you."

And he took it and fell silent.

But nobody seems to notice the slightest fraud. Why is the doctor getting out of the dust as quickly as possible? In the end, does he fear the discovery of his inability and, worse, of his wrong intentions?

II.3.2   The Neighbor

Franz Kafka, stories from the inheritance

My business lies completely on my shoulders. [3] Two misses with typewriters and business books in the lobby, my room with desk, cash box, consultation table, club chair, and a telephone, that's my whole working apparatus. So easy to survey, so easy to handle. I am quite young and the business runs along for me. I don't complain, I do not complain.

Since New Year, a young man has rented on the spot the small, vacant apartment next door, which for too long, I have unluckily hesitated to rent. Too, a room with a lobby, but additionally a kitchen.—I could have used the room and the lobby— my two misses sometimes felt overloaded already,—but which purpose would the kitchen have served for me? This petty concern was to blame that the apartment has been taken away from me.

Now this young man is sitting there. His name is Harras. I don't know what he's actually doing there. On the door is written: "Harras, Bureau". I have made inquiries, I was told that it is a business similar to the mine. One cannot warn against granting a loan, because it is a young, aspiring man whose cause may have a future, but one cannot really recommend granting a loan, because at the moment there is apparently no fortune.

---

[3]The English title is *My Neighbor*.

The usual information that one gives when not knowing anything. Sometimes I meet Harras on the stairs, he always has to be in a hurry, literally he rushes past me. I haven't seen him yet closely, he has already the office key prepared in his hand, and he is immediately opening the door. Like a rat's tail, he is slipping in, and I am left standing in front of the sign 'Harras, Bureau', which I have read much more often than it deserves.

The miserably thin walls that betray the honest man but cover the dishonest one. My phone is attached to the wall of the room that separates me from my neighbor. But I only emphasize this as a particularly ironic fact. Even if it would hang on the opposite wall, one would hear everything in the apartment next door. I have taken the habit to avoid telling the name of the customer on the phone. But of course, it doesn't take much cunning to guess the names from characteristic, but inevitable expressions of the conversation.—Sometimes I dance, with the phone at my ear, driven by restlessness, on the tips of my feet around the apparatus, and yet I cannot prevent secrets from being revealed.

Of course, this makes my business decisions shaky, my voice trembling. What is Harras doing while I am on the phone? If I would like to exaggerate very much—but one often has to do it to gain clarity—I could say: Harras doesn't need a phone, he uses mine. He has moved his sofa to the wall and listens. Whereas, I have to get to the phone, when it is ringing. I have to accept the customer's wishes, make important decisions, carry out large-scale persuasions,—but especially involuntarily, I have to report to Harras through the wall.

Perhaps, he does not even wait until the end of the conversation. After the point of the conversation sufficiently informing him about the case, he rises himself and scurries through the city, according to his habit. And before I hung up the ear-cup, he is perhaps already working against me.

Remark. Watch the live performance at:

`https://youtu.be/5CPZhCFF4GO`

II.3.3 About Kafka's Story *The Neighbor*

Sigmund Freud's interpretation of dreams can be read free of charge on *Projekt Gutenberg*.

Hello Hans-Peter,

I tried to read your Freud excerpt ... Well, I only understood what I had heard about it already before. Plenty of complications. I like the Greek legends better. And how the Bible explains dream interpretation. I found Kafka's story *The neighbor* on a CD. When you call up the CD track rip you get an mp4 file downloaded. I'll send it to you. Write me if you can play it.

—Greetings Franz

Dear Franz,

Thanks for the answer, which is similar to the one I received from Hanno. Kafka's story *The neighbor* has been the subject of one of my weekend seminars with Sam Weber (1996). At that time we talked about the "unsecret" in Freud, an eerie state full of ambivalence. Indeed, the "secretly homely" or "homely secret"—by looking more closely always turns out to be an "unhomely secret", getting more and more scary. Compare Freud's corresponding article. The seminar stood under the impression of the death of Emmanuel Levinas, an important Talmud specialist and discussion partner of Jacques Derrida. A reference to Kafka appears in Sam Weber's 2010 essay, which I attach for you. Even if I suspect, uncannily said that you understand it even less than Sam Weber's *tertium datur*.

The important issue about the story *The neighbor* is its relation to the DEATH which is always close to us as a scary guest (at the table, on the bed and at other occasions) and never allows us to be rejected. Such a symbol also appears in other places in Kafka's work, for example in the shape of *Odradek* in *The Care of the Housefather*. This "object" is also depicted in one of Jeff Wall's most famous art photos, my favorite photo artist.

—Lghp

Hello Hans-Peter,

Isn't this little story a wonderful parable for competition in business, as it is always lurking in the background; similarly in science, and in all types of working environments? If one looks at the story in this way, it gives a little comfort and amusement.

All the best Franz

Dear Franz,

Your approach to interpretation is justifiable, provided one applies it to the world of employment and the capitalist administration as a whole (see the work of sociologist Max Weber and above all the study by Siegfried Kracauer: The employees, 1929). Kafka was an employee of the workers' accident insurance company and a German Jew in Prague. With his illness, the overpowering loyalty to his father, and his crashed love affairs (especially Milena and Felicia Bauer) he was, so to speak, the successor to Herman Melville's *Bartleby*. Too, see Kafka's *Land Surveyer*, *Famine Artist*, *Josefine*. You always find him seeking for hope in writing. It was a life "directed towards death", as maybe Heidegger would have said. Neither being a valued citizen nor a really poor labourer, he was trapped between the classes of citizens and workers, as a foreign, alienated, part of the absurd life. Do you call that "amusing"? But for Kafka it was probably deadly serious: "Life . . . is only as long as the time you lose" I would say reflecting on his despair.

—Lghp

Hello Hans-Peter,

When I say "amusing" for my response to this story, the cat hatched from the sack. It becomes obvious how comfortably I have already settled into my retirement perspective. Many years ago, I, too, was typewriting in a tiny office, or sucked too little useful knowledge out of my fingers. I probably wouldn't have told my offspring that I am amusing myself with the paranoid competitive pressure that is shown as a caricature in this Kafka story.

—Greetings Franz

Dear Franz,

Thanks you again for your comments and your "joke!" And since I have just tried to clarify Sam Weber's article about *tertium datur* in my own words, I send it to you for review. Maybe you will discover something new in it?—Too, I find the problem with the cat exciting, because I am concerned with the problem of distinguishing animal and human; or with Jacques Derrida's words: "And if the animal could answer?" (Derrida was a passionate cat lover, too.)

—Lghp

Remark (Another opinion). But the competition is only the obvious problem of the text, the real problem is a deeper uncertainty and anxiety. Hesitancy, pettiness, distrust, anxiety, self-blame and obsessions shape his existence.—The text shows the genesis of prejudice and paranoia.

Part III

About My Father

Dr. Horst Rothe zum Andenken

Horst Rothe, Franz Rothe, Thomas Turner

Horst Rothe hat in persönlichen Gesprächen immer wieder die Bedeutung seiner Auslandsreisen, nach Java und viele Male USA, sowie die Veröffentlichung seines mehrbändigen Werkes über Elektronenröhren zusammen mit Walter Kleen, für seinen beruflichen Werdegang betont. Er hat mehr als zehn Doktoranten und ungezählte Diplomanten betreut.

Für den durch Krieg so verspäteten beruflichen Erfolg war mein Vater sehr dankbar. Schwere Krankheiten, auch seiner Ehefrau haben ihn ab 1962 zu einer viel zurückgezogeneren Lebenswese gezwungen als seinem lebhaften und kontaktfreudigen Wesen eigentlich entsprach. 1967 übernahm Prof. Dr. techn. Gerhard K. Grau die Leitung. Ab 1971 nennt es sich Institut für Hochfrequenztechnik und Quantenelektronik.   *Franz Rothe*
2019

Horst Rothe (1899-1974)

1 Rede zum 25. Jubiläum

Ralph Vaughan Williams (1872-1958)

2 Suite de Ballet (1924)
  I. Improvisation. Andante II. Humoresque. Presto
  III. Gavotte. Quasi lento IV. Passepied. Allegro vivacissimo
  Franz Rothe *Flöte*, Thomas Turner *Klavier*

III.0.1 Captured by High-frequency Electronics

`Dear friends,`

Hopefully, my two CDs in the mail will meet some interest. What happens to the "old recordings from adolescence" has not yet been decided. In any case, this CD should of course also be carried on with word of mouth to mouth propaganda. The other CD "Dr. Horst Rothe in Memory" contains the speech that my father held in 1952 at his 25th jubilee as director of the development department of the Telefunken company. This CD is available online from CD-universe

```
https://www.cduniverse.com/
productinfo.asp?pid=12375664&style=music
```

and on my website

```
https://www.franzrothe.com
```

On the front of the CD as well as in this little book, you can see the most appealing photograph of my father that I still own. You can feel all the natural vitality that has enabled him to achieve exceptional professional success during his long time at Telefunken, and which is also mentioned in his anniversary speech and my short biography. From the 25th jubilee around 1952, I for my part can remember only very little. As it sometimes happens, I was most surprised to see a pineapple for the first time. The parties with my parents in Ulm were joyful and lively, quite good wines were tasted. Here is a first excerpt from the anniversary speech:

> If today I can look back on twenty-five years at the company, I have to tell you that my coexistence with the electronic tube is actually almost 35

years old. Since it was in 1918 when I was a soldier lying in the war hospital at Namur when one day a soldier from the communications division came to me and asked:

"Listen, you're a student, and you have to actually know that. We have just gotten a new apparatus, and there is such a glass bulb on top, and a filament burns inside, and otherwise, there should be "nothing" inside. And what is it in reality?"

I could only mysteriously shake my head and say: "my dear comrade, I also know nothing." And it only became clear to me long afterwards that with the phrase "nothing in it" he obviously meant the word "high vacuum", of which we both had no idea at the time. At that time I could not have foreseen that a few years later, I joined Professor Barkhausen's laboratory at the Technical University in Dresden. And there I happened to me what Dr. Pietschik describes in such nice words and for which I am very grateful to him and to my dear employees: I found a personality, who cast a spell over me in the first minute where I saw him.

And through this encounter with Professor Barkhausen, it was decided at once in the first minute that I fell victim to low-voltage technology. Because I did not leave this institute during my time as a student and spent extremely happy years there. And it was another coincidence that finally tied me to the electronic tube: one day after I had worked in his institute only since a few days, Professor Barkhausen put a tube into my hand, in which there was again such a filament and otherwise "nothing", and asked: "Listen, what is it actually?" At that time we had already learned that the word "nothing" can be disguised under the fine term "high vacuum". But I hadn't learned what else was in it: it was the first oxide cathode tube that was freshly imported from America. At that time in Germany, we only had the glow cathode tube with tungsten thread. And the behavior of this oxide cathode tube was such a mystical one in all its characteristics that no one in the institute could get an idea about it.

From this work, my dissertation on oxide cathodes and a whole series of other publications emerged. And I like to think just as much as Dr. Heine here has told us, back to these years in Dresden, where one proceeded with leisure, but on the other hand with a sacred enthusiasm, I would like to say ...

My father had prevailed amid a company's tough struggle for survival. From the point of view of the bosses, his scientific foresight, it may seem to me, was only a less important matter compared to the success that primarily counted there. But in my father's view, humming and shaky contacts in the construction of electronic devices were only ridiculous little trifles, to be neglected in comparison to the deep insights into molecular physics that the phenomena of the *noise* mediates.

Only hard work, and especially the developments after the Second World War, fully confirmed his early technical and physical insights. In the end, even the cosmic background radiation shows that *noise* can be used to measure most precisely and investigate a lot of new things. My father had always said something similar concerning electronic tubes. An insight of my father regarding the construction of electron tubes is thus confirmed in an analogous manner even on an astronomical scale about cosmology.

I do not forget to mention that my father was a practical,

highly talented engineer. This was the time for rapid progress in the development of electronic tubes with several grids, like pentodes, hexodes, octodes. The more and more common use of high-frequency communications brought the necessity of amplification with increasing bandwidth at higher and higher frequencies. Beginning in 1933 Horst Rothe and Werner Kleen were developing the universal pentode RV12P2000.

In addition to the noble science, he was never averse to clever tricks. The following anecdote was only brought to me much later. In the 1930s, he developed at Telefunken the universal pentode, which was used in many of the receivers and transmitters of that time. The fairly bulky tube led to quite strong losses and disturbances due to direct high-frequency radiation. Contrary to the common usage, my father has now had the tube mounted with the anode down near the electrically conductive chassis. This trick significantly reduced the problem of radiation loss. Here is a second excerpt from the anniversary speech:

> My dear friends, a human's life is not only determined by these circles in which professional life takes place. And that I was happy and satisfied in this professional circle for these twenty-five years, I owe not only to all of you and your friendship and cooperation, but I owe it as well, or it is just as necessary to make this professional circle harmonious and in good shape, it is just as necessary that every person also creates his personal sphere in the same harmony and order. And this confronts us personally today with constantly rising and more difficult conflicts. Dr. Heine said in his words that the demands placed on us today, and indeed have to bet be made, are so strong that our personal life is neglected in many of these cases. And thus we get into an ever-growing conflict and recurring problems.

How can we devote ourselves enough to our family, how can we gain the time to get back the inner peace. I know, I think, I can say that I personally sinned a lot in these twenty-five years, perhaps because I often put a particular strain on my personal sphere caused by intervening scientific problems. I know, when I ponder about scientific problems, like Dr. Pietschik already said, when I come back to the office after Saturday and Sunday, and have recapitulated through these problems all weekend long, then I actually always have neglected my personal sphere. And here I think, ladies and gentlemen, allow me to express this personal thanks, and here I believe I have to pay a very big "thank you" to my dear wife.

If I had not had *your* help (applause) and understanding during this work to such an extent in these twenty years that we have been living together, and if *you* hadn't always managed to overlook the fact that I don't have time when I'm dealing with such a scientific problem, I think I would have, I could not have solved these questions. I believe that at such times when I am pondering such a scientific problem, especially in the eyes of a woman, I am sometimes a terrible disgust. So I sincerely ask for understanding from all you here, and I am deeply grateful that *you* have helped me in this sense these years.

My dear friends, allow me, forgive me for this deviation. But I think it to be part of the review, too, when one looks back on twenty-five years of life; and it is such an essential part of our life that we cannot take it into account enough. And I hope that we will succeed, will be able to promote this side of life more strongly and to take it in account more than we have been able to do so far.

III.0.2   Success After the War

Since 1945, Dr. Rothe has been the director of the laboratories of the entire electronic tube section at Telefunken. Under his responsibility, the development of electronic was rebuilt after the war from almost zero. Thus he has substantially contributed to the economic success of the company.

Too, he fabricated at that time the least noisy low-frequency transistor. During the years 1950-1955 he published together with several collaborators a number of investigations about noise in electronic tubes and, more generally, active network representation of noisy two-ports. He created together with W. Dalke the diagrams for noisy two-ports that has become generally accepted. For his work about the matrix representation, he has been appointed a fellow of the american IEEE.

In 1954 was founded at the technical university of Karlsruhe a professorship for electronic communications. where on April first of 1956, Prof. Dr.-Ing. Horst Rothe was appointed full professor. His appointment as a full professor at the TH Karlsruhe finally freed him from the many small conflicts in his former company, and it enables him to effectively propagate his general and far-sighted ideas about the science of high-frequency technology. In 1958, he founded the Institute for high-frequency electronics and physics.

At the invention of the maser in the early 50s, a quantum amplifier with a noise temperatur of a few degrees Kelvin, Rothe with his speciality in electronic noise engaged himself in this new domain. A short time later, the institute for highest frequency engineering and electronic was founded under Helmut Friedburg (* 1913). Both institutes worked together on the noise behavior of many types of amplifiers.

During personal communications, Prof. Rothe has continued to stress the importance of mainly two aspects for his professional success: travelling abroad to Java und many times the US, as well as the publication of his many volumes work about electronic tubes, together with Walter Kleen. He has taught more than ten Ph. D. students and countless master theses. My father was very thankful for his success, which came so late because of the war. In 1967 Prof. Dr. techn. Gerhard K. Grau took over as director of the institute. Since 1971, it is called the Institute for photonics and quantum electronics.

III.0.3   Health Problems

However, fate has intervened mercilessly, soon after these professional successes, serious illnesses have put a considerable strain on himself and his wife. Since his move to Karlsruhe, social contacts had become already sparser, and now they were almost completely stopped.

An exception were the old acquaintances from my parents prewar Berlin time, particularly the theater people,—the Rottler. Lizi Rottler was an opera singer, and her husband continued working as an intendant at the *Badisches Staatstheater*. Her daughter Marlies was just training to become an opera singer. Around the same time we met the student Klaus Rudolf Schubert, after he had shown himself interested to spend sometimes a Sunday with us and to discuss mathematics or physics with me, who was at this time attending the seventh grade. For me, this was the beginning of a lifelong friendship. More importantly, Rothe's house has mediated a marriage, as the reader may have speculated a little hastily. These are roughly the background for the two CDs that I have put together from the few remaining remnants of this old age and some newer ones.

Part IV

About Pianist Thomas Turner and Some Flute Music

IV.1 The CDs with Pianist Thomas Turner

Since childhood, I have become more and more familiar playing the flute. For a small concert that I had organized in the church of Wolfartsweier, a village near my home town Karlsruhe, I have performed together with Marlies Schubert Händel's German aria *Meine Seele hört im Sehen* ("My soul hears in seeing"), HWV 207. Unfortunately, this is the only recording of the many musical activities during my youth.

I have continued my musical training in North Carolina. During the years 1992 - 2003 a repertoire was practiced together with the pianist Thomas Turner, and three CDs have been recorded. See the covers for *Withered Flowers, Serenade* and *Mandoline* shown on pages 85, 86 and 87 below. These recordings were possible through the vigorous encouragement of Thomas and pianist Heather Coltman as well as flutists Irene Maddox and William Bennett. These were golden years for the musicians Rothe, and maybe Thomas, too.

I feel myself imitating the old boarding director Sesemi Weichbrodt from the *Buddenbrooks*, who nicely repackaged her old stuff for Christmas and gave it away again. For me with my poor eyesight, all flute playing is an activity from the past, as disintegrated as the *Buddenbrooks* family of Thomas Mann.

Nevertheless, I would like to invite you to listen to my last package of two CDs, which was released in November 2019.

A Bouquet Inspired From Songs and Instrumental Music

The list of pieces can also be seen in this little book. The CDs are available online at CDuniverse

```
https://www.cduniverse.com/
productinfo.asp?pid=12304490&style=music
```

and many other places, and on my website

https://www.franzrothe.com

Today from a distance, this collection from the golden years of Rothe and Turner amazes me with its forceful and accurate performance. Professional suppleness is almost achieved. The collection includes some almost forgotten pieces and surprises with (of course, less well-known) own transcriptions.

IV.1.1 Comments about These Pieces of Music

The following explanations are beginning with my own recordings, but are not limited to my own possibilities. Additionally, some hints to the many first-class recordings of these pieces are given. Perhaps this gives the reader one or the other suggestion for a gift.

Schubert Songs

The songs *Ständchen* (also called Serenade) and *Das Fischermädchen* (The Fishing Maiden) are number 4 and number 10 of Schubert's cycle *Schwanengesang*, D 957. The arrangements for the flute were composed by Theobald Böhm, the designer of the modern flute. They are virtuoso playful fantasies about these songs.

FRANZ ROTHE, FLUTE and THOMAS TURNER, PIANO
"Withered Flowers"   Music for flute and piano

LUDWIG VAN BEETHOVEN
(1770-1827)
1 **Rondo in G major,** WoO 41   [4:04]
(arranged for flute by F. Rothe)
Allegro

MAURICE RAVEL
(1875-1937)
2 From the Suite **"Ma mère l'oye"** [3:50]
(arrangement by Th. Turner)
Pavane de la belle au bois dormant
Petit poucet
3 **Pavane pour une infante défunte** [5:03]

GEORGE-ADOLPHE HÜE
(1858-1948)
4 **Sérénade**   [1:50]
Allegretto leggiero

CAMILLE SAINT-SAËNS
(1835-1921)
5 **Romance**   [4:31]
Moderato assai

ROBERT SCHUMANN
(1810-1856)
Three Romances, op. 94
6 Nicht schnell Moderato   [3:15]

7 Einfach, innig Semplice, affettuoso   [4:02]
8 Nicht schnell Moderato   [4:01]

RALPH VAUGHAN WILLIAMS
(1872-1958)
9 **Suite de Ballet** (1924)   [6:03]
Improvisation Andante-Poco piu mosso-Andante
Humoresque Presto
Gavotte Quasi Lento
Passepied Allegro vivacissimo

FRANZ SCHUBERT
(1797-1827)
10 **Introduktion und Variationen,** op. 160 [17:41]
über "Ihr Blümlein alle" aus den Müllerliedern
Introduktion Andante
Thema "Trockne Blumen" Andantino
Variationen I-VII

TOTAL PLAYING TIME: [54:46]

STEREO [D] [D] [D]
Ⓟ© 1998 Franz Rothe
Recording: Charles Vaughn
Photos: Luz Maria Aveleyra and Franz Rothe
Piano: Steinway & Sons
Flute: Johann Hammig, Freiburg i. Br.

Serenade

*Music
for
Flute
and
Piano*

Franz
Rothe, Flute

Thomas
Turner, Piano

"Serenade" Music for flute and piano
FRANZ ROTHE, FLUTE and THOMAS TURNER, PIANO

CHRISTOPH WILLIBALD GLUCK
(1714-1787)
1 From the Opera **"Orfeo"** [4:30]
The Dance of the Blessed Spirits

LUDWIG VAN BEETHOVEN
(1770-1827)
Serenade op. 41
2 Entrata Allegro [3:16]
3 Tempo ordinario d'un Menuetto [3:45]
4 Allegro molto [2:15]
5 Andante con Variazioni [5:39]
6 Allegro scherzando e vivace [1:57]
7 Adagio, Allegro vivace e disinvolto [5:42]

BENJAMIN GODARD
(1849-1895)
8 From **"Scotch Scenes"** [5:30]
Legende Pastorale Andante quasi adagio

GABRIEL-URBAIN FAURÉ
(1845-1924)
9 Les Berceaux Andante [2:46]
10 Sylvie Allegro moderato [2:56]

ROBERT SCHUMANN
(1810-1856)
Fantasy Pieces, op. 73
(transcription for flute F. Rothe)
11 Zart und mit Ausdruck [3:09]
12 Lebhaft, leicht [3:33]
13 Rasch und mit Feuer [4:28]

TOTAL PLAYING TIME: [49:30]
STEREO D D D
Ⓟ Ⓒ 2000 Franz Rothe
Recording: Charles Vaughn
Piano: Steinway & Sons
Flute: Johann Hammig, Germany

"Mandolin" SONG TRANSCRIPTIONS
FRANZ ROTHE, FLUTE and THOMAS TURNER, PIANO

FRANZ SCHUBERT (1797-1827)
transcriptions for flute by Theobald Boehm

1	Serenade	[4:50]
	Ständchen Moderato	
2	The Fishing Maiden	[2:26]
	Das Fischermädchen Allegretto	
3	The Carrier Pigeon	[3:50]
	Die Taubenpost Andante con sentimento	
4	The Linden Tree	[3:47]
	Der Lindenbaum Moderato	

GABRIEL FAURÉ (1845-1924)

5	The Cradles	[2:43]
	Les Berceaux Andante	
6	Sylvie Allegro moderato	[2:54]

CLAUDE DEBUSSY (1862-1918)

7	Romance Andante	[1:55]
8	Beautiful Evening	[2:16]
	Beau soir Andante ma non troppo	
9	Flowers of the Grainfield	[1:52]
	Fleur des blés Andantino moderato	
10	Here is Spring	[2:16]
	Voici que le printemps Andantino	
11	Mandolin Allegretto	[1:25]

MANUEL DE FALLA (1876-1946)
Siete Canciones populares Españolas
transcription by Thomas Turner

12	The Moorish Cloth	[1:21]
	El paño moruno Allegretto vivace	
13	Seguidilla from Murcia	[1:10]
	Seguidilla murciana Allegro spiritoso	
14	From Asturia	[1:59]
	Asturiana Andante tranquillo	
15	Jota Allegro vivo	[3:03]
16	Lullaby	[1:32]
	Nana Calmo e sostenuto	
17	Song	[1:05]
	Canción Allegretto	
18	Polo Vivo	[1:29]

TOTAL PLAYING TIME: [42:35]

Ⓟ Ⓒ 2003   Franz Rothe
Recording: Charles Vaughn
Cover photo: Alice Mayer
STEREO | D | D | D |

A Bouquet *inspired from songs and instrumental music*
Franz Rothe *flute and piano*, Thomas Turner *piano*, Andrea Hauk *flute*

Beethoven, Schubert, Fauré, Godard, Debussy,
Schumann, Saint-Saëns, Bozza, Poulenc, Baksa

Franz Rothe *flute and piano*,
Thomas Turner *piano*,
Andrea Hauk *flute*

A Bouquet Inspired by Songs

Franz Schubert (1797-1827)
1 Serenade *Moderato*
2 The fisher maiden *Allegretto*

Ludwig van Beethoven (1770-1827)
3 "To the far beloved" op.98 (1816)

Gabriel Fauré (1845-1924)
4 The cradles *Andante*

Eugène Bozza (1905-1991)
5 Aria (1971) *alto flute*

Claude Debussy (1862-1918)
6 Romance *Andante alto flute*
7 Here is spring *Andantino*
8 Mandolin *Allegretto*

Robert Baksa (*1938)
Flute sonata (1976)
9 *Allegro Cadenza I Adagio*
10 *Cadenza II Allegro*

A Bouquet from Classics

Ludwig van Beethoven
1 Rondo in G-major WoO 41

Benjamin Godard (1849-1895)
2 Legende Pastorale from "Scotch Scenes"
Andante quasi adagio

Ludwig van Beethoven
3 Rondo a capriccio in G, op.129
"The rage over the lost penny"

Camillie Saint-Saëns (1835-1921)
4 Odelette in D-major, op.162

Robert Schumann (1810-1856)
Fantasy pieces, op. 73
5 tender and expressive
6 lively, light 7 vivid and with fire

Eugène Bozza (1905-1991)
8 Aria (1971) *flute*

Francis Poulenc (1899-1963)
9 Sonata for flute and piano (1957)
Allegro malinconico Cantilena Presto giocoso

Beethoven's Song Cycle *"To the Distant Beloved"*, *Opus 98*

This work by Beethoven is less well known than Schubert's famous song cycles, which were created a little later. It is also a little easier to master. You can hear my own production, sung and accompanied by myself, one person does double work. Beethoven's song cycle was a stimulating role model for Franz Schubert. The interested listener can certainly find excellent recordings.

Gabriel Fauré

Gabriel Fauré (1845-1924) was one of the most productive song composers in France at the turn of the century. The song *Les berceaux*, Opus 23, number 1 (in English: The Cradles), weeps and sings the pain of separation of sailers when they have to set sail and leave back women and children at home.

Eugène Bozza, Aria for Alto Flute and Piano

This piece is already originally available in several versions: in a very high pitch for violin or flute and in a lower pitch for clarinet, or even for alto saxophone. I transposed the piece myself into a pitch for alto flute. In addition, I have produced a second version for flute in a more convenient pitch that can be heard here, too. I have rewritten the piano part with the aim of making it easier to play. Under the keyword "Bozza Aria" you will find on the internet many recordings on the most varied instruments.

Claude Debussy

We can hear on my CDs from the "Eight Early Songs" :
Romance, played with alto flute and piano,
Here is spring, and mandolin, played with flute and piano.

Robert Baksa

Robert Baksa was born in New York City in 1938 and is of Hungarian descent. He is one of the most productive American composers. One of his earliest works for flute is the Flute Sonata Number 1. It was created in 1976 but was only premiered in the late 1980s. It is among the winners of the 1994 "Newly Published Music Competition",—a prize donated by the "National Flute Association".

The movements are: Allegro, Cadenza I, Adagio, Cadenza II, Allegro

Beethoven, *Rondo in G major, WoO 41*

Here you can hear my own transcription from violin to flute.

Benjamin Godard, *Legend pastoral* from the cycle "Scotch Scenes"

Beethoven, *Rondo a Capriccio in G, Opus 129*

Beethoven composed this hit in 1795. The piece rightly has the nickname "Rage Over a Lost Penny". This fiery composition made me have a lot of fun playing. Thomas still writes to me:

> Franz, the two CDs arrived yesterday. Thank you very much! I haven't listened to them yet, but I'll do it soon. In any case, I think you should clarify *who* is playing Beethoven's *Rondo a Capriccio, Opus 129*. This is the only way the listener can know for sure. I assume you play it, but of course, it could be the second flautist, who knows? You really put some of our best pieces on the CDs!

Many excellent recordings of this hit are on the internet under the title "Rage Over a Lost Penny".

Robert Schumann

The three movements of the fantasy pieces, Opus 73, are already by Schumann titled in German.
Zart und mit Ausdruck (Delicate and with expression);
Lebhaft, leicht (Lively, light);
Rasch und mit Feuer (Quick and with fire).

Robert Schumann has written the fantasy pieces Opus 73 in a version for cello and piano, - as well as a version for clarinet and piano. For my own adaptation for flute, I only had to choose the appropriate octave in the melody part. The sharper articulation of the syncope at the beginning of the third movement, which is more suitable for the flute, is taken over by Schumann's cello version.

Eugène Bozza

Aria for Flute and Piano is set a little lower and more comfortably than the original version. The listener may compare.

Francis Poulenc

Sonata for Flute and Piano: Allegro malinconico, Cantilena, Presto giocoso.
Of Francis Poulenc's *Flute Sonata* there exist many excellent recordings, starting with the original from 1957, played by the world famous flutist *Jean-Pierre Rampal* and the composer.

https://m.youtube.com/watch?v=OaIeWmZBUL8

https://www.youtube.com/
watch?v=OaIeWmZBUL8&app=desktop

https://www.youtube.com/watch?v=2TOZv7rPPfo

Among the more recent recordings I was impressed by

- Poulenc : Sonate pour Flute et Piano etc.
  Mathieu Dufour Released 12/15/2010 — 1:00:56

- Poulenc: Flute Sonata
  by William Bennett, Clifford Benson — 13 Tracks — 59:22
  Released 2003

- Debussy - Poulenc - Ravel - Roussel: Musique française
  pour flûte by Sandrine Piau; Patrick Gallois; Jean-Pierre
  Rampal; Emile Naoumoff — 13 Tracks — 1:08:19 Released
  2012

IV.1.2   My Adaption with Two Flutes

The concert piece *Odelette* in D major, Opus 162 (in English "Small Ode"), is a late work by Camille Saint-Saens (1835 - 1921). It was composed in 1920, and was originally set for flute and orchestra. The piece has a clearcut structure and is based on a melody of classic, even Greek flavor. The flute part is rich in playful and virtuoso ornaments. I got to know this piece around 1998, during the years when I played regularly together with pianist Thomas Turner. The simple and at the same time playful character of the piece did attract me immediately.

While the flute part is demanding, putting everything together seemed to be rewarding enough and within our abilities. But Thomas was very reserved, especially because of the transcription for piano. This transcription contains several passages with only a single melody line for the piano. This is very unusual and awkward for any pianist since it does allow the piano sound to develop naturally.

Instead of insisting on practicing the flute and piano version, I set about rewriting the piece for two flutes and piano. The simple classic style of the piece gave me confidence in such an endeavor. In the version for flute and piano, there already exist variations with the character of a duet. On top of that, the long virtuoso runs were much easier to master by distributing them on two flutes. These properties of the composition make the transcription for two flutes a natural undertaking. Of course, there did arise additional problems during this endeavor. Indeed it became necessary to invent some additional parts of figured bass and to redistribute voices. After a few months of such work, I managed to get a transcription. We have played it together with Andrea as the second flautist and Thomas as pianist.

I have sent the recording to a music publisher. Thanks to mediation, the manuscript has been accepted and is now available from the online sources: allflutesplus, and: justflutes.

```
https://www.allflutesplus.com/product/
saint-saens-odelette-opus-162-two-flutes-and-piano
-alry/
```

```
https://www.justflutes.com/
charles-camille-saint-saens-odelette
-product1406702.html
```

Here is a review by Chris Hankin from the staff of "Just Flutes": Staff Pick *Music for Friends*

> What could be nicer than making good flute music with a few friends, especially a piece that you have already studied as a solo? This arrangement is appealing, captures all the colors and liveliness of Saint-Saens original, but distributes the load to two players. The piano part has been simplified to give the flutes more to do. The overall effect is retained. A great addition to the repertoire for two flutes. You will like it!

In addition, there exists now a recording with two first-class flutists on their CD.

Luminance by Lisa Friend, Anna Stokes, Mark Kinkaid Released 2014, Champs Hill Records.

Here is criticism from Amazon.

> I have bought this wonderful CD for my daughter be-
> cause I thought it would inspire her and improve
> her own flute playing and practicing. I couldn't
> have chosen a more suitable CD. She listened to it
> again and again and is now practicing like crazy.
> My daughter and I are completely in love with
> the cover picture, and the flute playing is just as
> beautiful.

In memory of my (small) contribution, I could imagine appearing in the background of the cover picture. For example, as a
dwarf sitting on a cloud, while I watch from a distance how the
clear flute tones, regularly like raindrops from two clouds, swell
from the mouths of the two nymphs.

The version for two flutes and piano from the CD *Luminance*
can be heard online on YouTube.

https://youtu.be/U1g2Xr9sTtc

The original version for flute and orchestra can also be heard on
YouTube.

https://youtu.be/i2EaLV2NhVY

https://youtu.be/c1K7Gx54NXs

https://youtu.be/qhNSJP57xwA

Finally, the version for one flute with William Bennett and piano
with Clifford Benson can be heard on YouTube.

https://youtu.be/JNbnOC9Ga54

IV.2 Life Goes on

IV.2.1 German Songs

All instrumental music remains rigid like a structure from stone, compared to the flexibility and natural vitality of the human voice. The listener has already got to know Marlies Schubert's youthful voice with Händel's German aria *Meine Seele hört im Sehen* ("My soul hears in seeing"), HWV 207. During her further career, Marlies not only devoted herself to the opera but also the German song, with especial emphasis on the work of female composers. In the songs "Schwanenlied", "Nacht Wanderer" and "Maienlied" by Fanny Mendelsohn you can literally feel the light and shadow of the German landscape. I enjoy hearing again and again, her recording together with Walter Landmann, piano.

IV.2.2 A Closing Word

Finally, two great writers are quoted for consolation and as a warning, both for the reader and also for me.

> He walked the path he had to take, a little careless and uneven, whistling to himself, looking sideways with his head bowed sideways, and if he went astray, it happened, because for someones there is no really correct way.
> —*Thomas Mann, Tonio Kröger*

In the end, the most suitable quote comes from old Goethe.

> Young man, remember in times,
> When mind and spirits rise:
> That to accompany the muse can,
> But conducting does not understand.
> —*Johann Wolfgang von Goethe*

Printed in the USA
CPSIA information can be obtained
at www.ICGtesting.com
LVHW062147280923
R17906000001B/R179060PG759108LVX00001B/1

* 9 7 8 1 6 8 4 8 6 4 5 6 0 *